Baptized by Fire
A Nurse's Story

Patricia Kline (Brantley) Nix

Acknowledgements

With a grateful heart I salute James Wyman Brantley Jr., my son and chief editor, who lit a fire and made it happen.

My two daughters, Melanie B. Murphy and Allison B. Carter, are my constant supporters and cheerleaders, and have been throughout this process.

To Rosemary Daniell, founder and leader of the Zona Rosa writing workshops based in Savannah, GA, I raise my glass. She reintroduced me to writing and handled my hesitations with care. I followed her around the world to partake of every morsel of her expertise. "The story is finally out of me!" Thanks you for your patience and T.L.C.

June B. Pugh. Professor, friend, author, and editor. How do I count the ways? You have lived this story with me from the beginning and have hung in there till the end. Many thanks for all of it, including feeding Jim during my absence.

Lee Ann Swanekamp. Thank you for your thoughtful editing and insight. Maybe my movie dreams will come true!

Bailey White. Author, friend, editor.   Your calm approach strengthened my determination to pursue my goal. Your advice guided me in the right direction. Thank you.

To all my friends and family who encouraged me on this journey, I am eternally grateful.

The descriptions of world events in this manuscript were informed by the following reference work: *Chronicle of the 20th Century,* edited by Clifton Daniel, John Kirshon, and Tod Olson. ECAM Publications, Inc. 1987 edition.

I was very young when my Dad and uncles went "off to war" during World War II. Their absence, however, was very real to me. Fortunately, they all returned safely. In my young eyes, they were my heroes.

This book is dedicated to all those who lived through it all with me, but who have gone on before to their ultimate rewards.

Pat Nix
Jesup, GA
2019

Prologue

"See the boots she's wearing, Shane? Those are combat boots."

"What's that around her neck, Mimi?"

"That's a stethoscope, Patrick. You know, like the doctor listens to your heart. I used one like that when I was a nurse in the Army."

"Well, what's she looking at, Mimi?"

"She's looking in the sky for a helicopter to come rescue the person who is hurt on the ground."

"Is that you, Mimi?"

As we sit on the National Mall in Washington, D.C., we gaze up at the Vietnam Women's Memorial. My granddaughter, Brantley, sits in her stroller. It is a quiet moment.

I try to explain its significance to my grandchildren. Thoughts of their future, memories of the price paid to be where we are today and the part of history played by the Vietnam War floods my mind.

After many more questions and my attempts to answer at their level of understanding, we continue our stroll. The Washington Monument looms in the distance. Its reflection glistens in the pool.

We loop around to the Vietnam Veterans Memorial Wall where I again try to explain an era that is so hard to understand.

Problems and Decisions

"Surely you see how practical this plan is," I plead. "I can finish these last two years of school without more loans piling up."

Jim's clear blue eyes cloud to gray as his brow furrows. He strokes his chin while digesting this information. "For you, but what about us?"

"Well, of course for us it means we can get married sooner since I get a monthly salary as well as paid tuition and books."

Since last Tuesday afternoon, when representatives from the Air Force, Navy and Army Nurse Corps visited the campus and talked to the student body at the school of nursing I have felt that this is my answer. This solution resolves two major problems in my life: paying for college and completing plans for marriage.

Despite our busy schedules I arrange to meet Jim for lunch in Cox Hall, the campus cafeteria, specifically to discuss the Army Nurse Program. His sophomore curriculum in Emory Medical School and mine in the Nursing School leaves us little time together, much less for serious discussion.

Since our meeting two and a half years ago at Emory-at-Oxford, my first quarter there and his last, our relationship continues to grow stronger. Talk of marriage now creeps into our conversations. These usually end when questions of finances arise. I must convince Jim that this program answers our problems. With the chatter from other students and the clang of dishes around us, I wonder about my choice of time and place.

"You say the Army pays your tuition, housing and a salary every month?"

"Yes, for the next two years. I'll owe them only three years of service in return."

I hold up three fingers and feel my eyes dance with excitement. I wish someone would turn that music down. "'I can't stop lovin' you-u-u. I've made up my mi-i-ind—to live in miser-ry,'" whines Ray Charles over the intercom.

Is it prophetic that our favorite song floods our ears as we discuss our future? For some reason, it's bothering me.

"But where would you be stationed?" Jim asks, running his hands through his wavy hair.

"If we're married, they try to station us together; so I could be here in Atlanta at Ft. McPherson. It's like having a job in a regular hospital."

"It could be dangerous," insists Jim.

"The last war was ten years ago--in Korea."

He rises to go. His lanky frame towering over me. Picking up my tray I follow his lead.

"I'm still not sold. Have you talked to your parents?"

"Not yet."

Jim purses his lips, shakes his head and mumbles, "I don't know. Sounds good on the surface. There must be some catch."

Still convinced that it's our solution, I have to decide how to approach Mother. I know it's not going to be easy. As an only child, I left for college the same year that my parents divorced, ending a 19-year marriage. Even though that was three years ago, Mother suffered two significant losses in one year. There is no perfect time nor place for this encounter.

❧❧

When I enter the cozy kitchen that is now her home Mother and I surround each other with hugs. Mother's face shines with pure delight. Her warm reception makes me feel sheepish for being there on this mission.

Sitting at the small kitchen table, dawdling over my cereal, I know that I have to broach the subject. Seeing the twinkle in Mother's eyes, I hesitate. She seems much happier these days since she met and married a genteel bachelor a couple of years after her divorce. I chew my fingernail while waiting for her reaction to my financial plans.

"You want to do what?" Mother whirls around from the sink, her hands dripping with soapy dishwater.

"I-I'm trying to find a way to make my educational finances easier."

"The only one I see it really helping is your Daddy. The one obligation left for him in the settlement was to send you to college. Why are you doing this? Have you talked to him?"

"No, ma'am, not yet."

It always amazes me how quickly I feel like a child again in Mother's presence especially if I think she disapproves.

"I don't like asking him for money all the time. I know tuition goes up every year at Emory. The last two quarters Dad and I applied for student loans together."

"Well, he'd better pay for those," counters Mother with a wave of her arm, as if dismissing the subject.

"Not necessarily," I reply, rising to take my bowl to the sink.   I turn to Mother to observe her reaction.   Even though I am several inches shorter I feel more adult at this level, more ready to face her,

"My name is the first one signed on those loans. I don't mind making some contribution."

"But the Army?   Are you sure this was not his idea?   This is a serious step."

Several days pass before I can arrange to see Dad. He plans to pick me up in front of the dormitory to go out for dinner at a small restaurant with home-style cooking. Any change is welcome from the institutional food even though the cafeteria-style gives lots of choices. Prompt, as usual, I watch as he maneuvers the small, white foreign car parallel to the curb. With a glance in the mirror I give one final touch to the brown hair that frames my face. Flying down the steps, I run like a kid at Christmas to meet him.

"How's my girl tonight?"

"Fine, but I'm worried about this biochem quiz. Think I should've stuck to my original dream of being a journalism major." I reach over to peck his cheek. "And how are you?"

Daddy remarried a short time after Mother; but, I am glad that he arrives alone tonight. During the short ride to Evan's Fine Food, a local cafe with home-style cooking, we chat with ease.

I relax as I notice that his mood seems upbeat. Settled at our table, with our orders given to the waitress, I explain the Army Nurse Program.

"That sounds interesting."

"Yes, and I think I'd be stationed right here in Atlanta!"

"You can't be sure what the Army will do."

"You were from Columbus, stationed at Ft. Benning while we lived there with Grandmother."

"That's true, honey, but I also went to Germany during World War II."

"Weren't you in the Intelligence Corps?"

"Yes, I was lucky.   Some of my buddies weren't.   That was a tough time," Dad replies, his eyes glazing over.

"Well, there's no war now," I shrug, trying to lighten the mood as I eat my lemon pie.

Dad reaches across the table, brushes my cheek and says, "I appreciate your wanting to help. I don't think I can let you do that. My little girl in the Army?   Incredible," shaking his head.

"Look how much help this would be with our finances," I say, pleading my case.

"Yes.   I also know there must be some other solution."

Though studying consumes most of my time, I manage to arrange an appointment with the recruiter. During this session she explains details of rank and salary. She assures me that special consideration in assignment is given to those who are married. I believe her. The decision is ultimately mine. She also mentions that if a nurse becomes pregnant she receives an immediate discharge from the Corps without further obligation.

What a loophole that is! Did I hear her right? The heavy feeling of aloneness lifts I am convinced that this last point will be my 'coup de gras.' What if my orders send me to another part of the country, or even another part of the world? Why, I can just get pregnant.

Jim looks astounded as I recount my conversation with the recruiter to him over dinner.

"You didn't sign anything, did you?"

"No just listen to me."

I reiterate, in detail, rank, salary and obligatory service. Finally, we arrive at the decision that the program answers our needs.

On April 5, 1962, I take the oath of induction into the United States Army with my mother, another recruit and her mother in attendance. A somber but cordial atmosphere hangs over the room, possibly a foreshadowing of events yet to come.

༻ৎৣঌ༺

In 1961, President Kennedy sends advisers to tour Vietnam. General Maxwell Taylor and Walt Roston recommend sending 8000 U. S. combat troops into the country. President Kennedy sends, instead, more equipment and advisers. By the end of 1961, the number of U. S. military personnel in Vietnam increases from 760 to 3205.

On February 6, 1962 the American Military Assistance Command (MACV) is formed and based in Saigon. In May of 1962, Marines (5000) and jets (50) fly to Thailand to prevent Communist expansion in Laos. American advisers in Vietnam increase to almost 12,000.

Choices and Assignment

July 28, 1963: "How do I look?   Is my veil on straight?"   I preen in the mirror as Nancy, my maid of honor reaches to fluff the netting, then kneels to adjust the blue garter as the camera flash causes me to blink again.

Our wedding day, we've planned and looked forward to it for about two years of the four that we've been dating.   Can it possibly be a reality?   This is the "big day."

"...to honor and to cherish in sickness and in health until death us do depart," pronounces the minister.   "You may now kiss your bride."

Then up the aisle and out the chapel doors we fly to meet our future as husband and wife. As we left the church we did not know that in less than two years we would experience the longest separation of our lives.

The days turn into months as each of us moves into the last year of our respective schools at Emory. My tuition and books are paid without a problem. No calling Dad to see if the money is there nor its source. The basic monthly allowance, as well as Jim's scholarships and extra jobs, provides us with a tight, but liveable income.

We live in a rented terrace apartment. In reality, the basement of a house with a private entrance opening onto the side of a sloping driveway. I can bike to school or be picked up by a classmate when our schedules do not coincide.

"Thanks for the ride, Judy. I'll see you tomorrow," I said, waving her off as I unlock our door.

Home early and alone, I turn on the television for company. While changing from my once crisp-now-limp navy blue and white student uniform, I notice figures in a motorcade moving across the screen. On this clear November day in Dallas, President John F. Kennedy and the First Lady ride in a convertible while crowds cheer and wave. I watch with rapt attention as their car rounds a corner in front of several large buildings.

"Pop, pop, pop!"

Was that gunfire? I look closer at the television screen as if I can see into it. I first see general commotion, then the limousine carrying the President, his wife, and Governor and Mrs. John Connally, veers off to the right and speeds away.

Shock washes over me when the announcement comes that the President has died. The torch passes on Air Force One as Lyndon Baines Johnson takes the oath of office of the President of the United States while Jacqueline Kennedy looks on in silence.

∾∾

In 1963, the Army of the Republic of South Vietnam experiences a huge defeat by the Vietcong at the Battle of Ap Bac. Buddhist monks stage anti-government demonstrations which bring them immediate reprisals. Numerous monks, in protest, commit suicide, publicly by setting themselves afire.

Several South Vietnamese officers, including General Duong Van Minh, overthrow the Diem government with United States knowledge and assistance from the C.I.A. Diem and his brother are murdered. President Kennedy is assassinated three weeks later.

The numbers increase. American advisers rise to 16,300 and U.S. monetary assistance to five hundred million. The C.I.A. begins a training program with South Vietnamese guerillas organizing a covert sabotage plan against the North Vietnamese under American oversight.

"Doctor James Wyman Brantley..." booms the Dean of the Emory Medical School.

Straining and stretching as high as possible I try to distinguish his face among a sea of black caps and flowing robes. His expression remains serious as he shakes hands, then moves the gold tassel from one side to the other.

The Nursing School graduates follow. As my name, Patricia Kline Brantley, resounds across the quadrangle a smile of pride and pure joy breaks across my face. Words of congratulations and the flashes of cameras follow the ceremony as our relatives and friends surround us. We move on to enjoy a huge celebration feast.

Last Monday Jim received notice that he begins a rotating internship on July1st with the Emory-Grady-Veterans Administration Hospitals. This program allows him to experience all areas of medicine. Then, at the year's end, he chooses his area of specialization. The competition for these positions is brutal, so we have extra reason to celebrate.

Following a short vacation at the beach we settle into a routine of working and more studying. State board exams loom ahead of us. We move to a small rental house about two miles from the hospital

"Do you think I've learned anything during all these years?" I ask Jim one day, slamming my book shut in frustration.

"You know you have, honey," he replies absently, pouring himself a glass of milk.

"I know, but can I recall the right stuff to regurgitate on this final challenge? You know I have to pass this to be able to practice as a registered nurse and to move on with my next step in the Nurse Corps, not to mention making a higher salary."

"I know. I have to pass mine, too."

❧❦

One day in mid-September, leaves tinged with gold, temperatures dropping, I check the mailbox as usual, returning from the 7 a.m. To 3 p.m. shift. There it sits, perched atop the pile, confirmation or rejection of my registered status. Will I have to repeat it? Can I move on with my career? I'm not sure that I want to open that envelope.

"Congratulations! You are a registered professional nurse #RP25164. Does R.N. stand for 'Real Nurse' now?" laughs Jim. We raise our glasses in celebration.

"Yes, and my next step is to notify the Army recruiting office."

Jim's blue eyes cloud.

"Do you have to do that?   The news reports don't sound too good.   There've been some attacks on one of our ships."

We both knew that the question was rhetorical. All medical personnel entering the Army must spend a six-week orientation period at Ft. Sam Houston in San Antonio, Texas at the Medical Field Service School.   It's located on the campus of Brooke Army Medical Center.   A mixture of excitement and sadness fills my thoughts. Six weeks—the longest time we will be apart since our first meeting in the snack bar on the Oxford campus.   Maybe this will be the only separation we'll have to endure.

"Yes, I did hear those reports; but surely they'll negotiate before any full-blown war occurs. Who's the best man for President, anyway?"

Early in 1964, Lieutenant General William Westmoreland is appointed deputy commander of Military Assistance Command (MACV).   In June of that year, he assumes the command of the same post.

In August of 1964, an American destroyer, the Maddox, is conducting electronic surveillance ten miles offshore of North Vietnam, in the Gulf of Tonkin. The Maddox is pursued by three North Vietnamese torpedo boats. As they move in closer the destroyer opens fire and the patrol boats respond with torpedoes, missing the Maddox.

The Maddox calls for air support from a carrier nearby and three American fighter planes attack the torpedo boats. The destroyer, Maddox, sinks one patrol boat, disables the other two and withdraws. Two days later the Maddox and the Turner Joy, another destroyer, are sent back to the Gulf to establish authority in the waters.

On this same day, President Johnson reports to congressional leaders that the Maddox sustained another attack. This was never confirmed and was proved later never to have occurred.

The next day, August 5, U. S. bombers retaliate for the "attacks" on U.S. ships, destroying oil depots and patrol boats. Two U. S. planes are shot down and the first American prisoner of war is captured. Everett Alvarez will be held captive for more than eight years. Two days later the House unanimously votes and the Senate has only two dissenting votes, to pass the Gulf of Tonkin Resolution.

It gives President Johnson any powers necessary to impede any further aggression. In September, United Nations Secretary U. Thant proposes to mediate talks with North Vietnam in order to settle the differences with the U. S.. Johnson does not receive complete information; therefore, the negotiations are rejected by the U. S.

On October 30, 1964, the U. S. airbase at Bien Hoa is attacked by the Vietcong. Six B-57 bombers are destroyed and five Americans are killed.

In November, President Johnson and Hubert Humphrey defeat Barry Goldwater, the Republican candidate, by a landslide. By December, the count of American military advisers rises to 23,300.

అసా

"Lieutenant, are you sure you polished that brass last night?"

"Yes, sir."

"Well, maybe you need another lesson in polishing."

"Yes, sir."

Welcome to the Army.

My class of nurses begin our "how-to" lesson in soldiering with enthusiasm. Our mornings are spent in class studying the hierarchy of the Army and, more specifically, the medical and nurse corps structure. We learn a new body of terminology, such as the structure of a field hospital versus an evacuation hospital.

We wear a uniform of dark green suit, hat (cover) and black heels, all exactly alike. Our issue of white uniforms is also the same. I can no longer wear my new Emory cap. Instead I have to wear one unique to the Army Nurse Corps. Individual style is stripped away.

Afternoons find us in formation marching, turning, about-facing, double-timing, saluting (when and how) and finally, "at ease," all done in the hot Texas sun.

On Thursday, during one of these sessions, the class settles into the repetitive drill.

"...left, right, left, right, left, right, abo-out 'ace, hut left, right..."

Since I am short, my usual position is on the end of a row so that there is no one in front of me when we march toward the west.

The afternoon sun beams like the new diamond on my left hand, permeates my uniform, warming my body to its core, mesmerizing my mind.

Even in November the temperature soars, compounded by the fact that we march on asphalt which radiates heat. The hypnotic effect dulls every fiber.

"Squadron—halt! Lieutenant, are you leaving or going with us?"

A muffled ripple of laughter floats over from the group. Only at that moment do I realize that there are no footsteps behind me. Apparently, I missed the command for ""about face." With brisk steps and a red face I resume my position.

"You think this stuff is hard to learn—just wait till we get to Camp Bullis," says Bob, the male nurse from Pennsylvania.

"I'll have another plate of those fries," motions Kathy, as we convene in the snack bar to rehash the day's activities.

"What's Camp Bullis?" I blurt.

"Oh, I heard about that place before I left home," says Mara, an attractive auburn-haired nurse from Wisconsin. "It's where you really learn to be a soldier in the field. Don't we go there during the fourth week here?"

All I want to be is a civilian nurse, home with Jim, I thought, making a mental note to discuss this later with Mara. This group probably includes some career Army who would be offended by my honesty.

There's a chill in the early morning air as the thick mist lifts like a shade rolling up on the window. We load our gear and ourselves into three-quarter ton trucks and head toward Camp Bullis.

"You better hope it doesn't rain while we're out here," warns one of the older guys. "They say it always rains at Bullis, as if by special order from the Army, if not all week, at least for part of it. We'll learn what it's really like to be in the trenches then."

"Yeah, well, it's only for a week. We're nurses. Most of this stuff we'll never use," pipes Betty.

"I've never touched an M-16 before, much less fired one," I announce as we settle into our own thoughts for the hour's ride.

"Humph, that'll change," comes an unknown voice from the group.

During the week, we all do things that we had never done and hope we never have to do again.   We learn to use our helmets, our maps and compasses.   We savor the taste of creamed beef on toast served up on metal plates with bread and beans from C-rations (canned food).   We dip our utensils and plates into a barrel of boiling water to wash them.   We follow the physical achievement course laid out for us.   We learn to live as a community in the field.   The mood is upbeat because we know the situation is not real and will end in a week.

We cheer as the trucks roll in to carry us back to our comfortable dormitory rooms and civilization.   We escape with only one day of rain.

"Lyndon Baines Johnson wins in a landslide election," announces Walter Cronkite, as we all listen in the day-room. It had been my first experience voting absentee ballot and my candidate had not won.

We all speculate on the future of our country. "'In your heart you know he's right.'" still rang in my ears from the Goldwater campaign blitz.

Thanksgiving leave brings a welcome break. I fly home, at our expense, for the traditional feast and the warmth of family.

On the return flight I think of the times I'm missing with those I love. The wedding of good friends that I could not attend. The daily talks with my Grandmother. I don't like this feeling of estrangement. What if I really do get sent to some faraway place? How will I handle it? What will my parents think of my decision then? Will our marriage survive it?

❦

"What did you put for your first assignment choice, Pat?" asked Bob, one morning at breakfast.

"Somebody told me to put my last choice first and vice-versa. Then I'll get my first choice in Atlanta at Ft. McPherson. I'm afraid to do that, though—what if I really put San Francisco first and got it? How would I ever explain that to Jim?"

The next two weeks are full of classes, more drills, tests and immunizations. We wait and wonder. Our fates hang in the balance.

"Do you ever get your first choice of assignment?" I ask Mara one night while discussing life's problems in her room. "I feel like nobody out there is looking out for my good, especially not that recruiter." Mara has a brother in the Army and seems more knowledgeable than some of us. "Sometimes I wish I were Becky."

Becky was a married member of our class for about a week and a half. She was tested at the clinic, determined positive for pregnancy, discharged and sent home. She never served another day in the Army. All that investment in her down the drain.

"I'm not sure my conscience would let me do that-even if I had a husband.

"Yeah, the Army has invested a lot in us. It is tempting, though."

"Pass another one of those pimento cheese sandwiches. Is that hot stuff jalapeno?" yells Bev.

"I guess it is. We're in Texas and that's close to Mexico."

"They're almost as good as that barbecued goat we had at that cook-out after Bullis," says Bob.

"This calls for another beer," rose a voice in the crowd.

The party rocks on as we celebrate our assignment orders and the close of our M.F.S.S. Class.

"Lieutenant Patricia Kline Brantley report to U.S. Army Hospital, Ft. McPherson, Georgia on December 20, 1964."

I blink back the tears of joy as I read and re-read the trembling paper in my hand. Maybe my family now will see the wisdom of my decision.

Orders and Arrival

The hospital plant, itself, consisted of a two-level structure of World War II vintage. The yellowed wood building looked old but well-kept. There was no medicinal smell, only a faint odor of pine. Various wings where patients were housed spread out like sorghum syrup on a hot pancake.

Sitting outside the door, labelled "Lt. Col. Florence Pecora, Chief Nurse," I heard her voice, clear, but clipped, honed from years in military service.

"Yes, tell Lt. Baker to be here at 1500 hours. She'll cover ward four. Thank you."

As soon as I hear the receiver click into its cradle I stand, a knot in my stomach, ready to execute a crisp salute, "Lt. Brantley reporting for duty."

"Good morning, Lieutenant, at ease. Come in and have a seat."

"'At ease.'"

Ha, how could anybody be 'at ease' in this office? I had heard that when one was summoned here the news was rarely good.

I told myself that I was only reporting for duty, so relax. I was sure she probably could read my thoughts behind the veneer of my smile.

"Welcome to Ft. McPherson, Lt. Brantley, I think you'll like our hospital."

"Thank you, I'm definitely glad to be here."

"You're assigned to ward three, the woman's ward. Sgt. Malick, the corpsman, will give you a tour of the facility before you go to your area. You need to fill out some papers first. Do you have any questions?"

"Not now, but I'm sure I'll have plenty later."

Lt. Col. rises and I follow her lead. "Right this way and you can begin."

∞∞

I settle with ease into my position on ward three to begin my Army career. The drive from Decatur to south Atlanta (25 miles) gets long and monotonous. It makes more sense for me to drive rather than Jim to make a long drive with his erratic hours.

One morning when I arrive for the 0700 shift the ward is abuzz with activity.

"Oh, thank goodness, you're here a little early. Good morning, Lt. Brantley," gushed Mrs. Sullivan, the civilian nurse, coming off the night shift.

"Good morning.   Is there a problem, Mrs. Sullivan?"

"No, no real problem, Lieutenant, but the Chief has already been by to tell us that someone will be admitted to our VIP suite today.   She wants us to be sure everything is clean and in order."

"Do we know the patient's name?"

"Not yet-someone mentioned a general's wife..."

Ward three consists of a large room with beds lining each side having only curtains between them for privacy.   The nurses' office contains two desks and the medicine cabinet.   It is an enclosed room with no view of the patients. Next door to the office is the kitchen/utility room, where the coffee pot causes staff to congregate between duties.   A few steps across the hall is the VIP suite and bath.   It's situated within easy access of the nurses' office in order to satisfy any immediate need.

For much of the day I direct the scrubbing and cleaning with regular duties and patient care interspersed. If anyone important appears we want to be ready. About 1400, the Chief Nurse came onto the ward. She literally was wearing white gloves. If any dust or dirt remained she was determined to find it. Of course, she found some--in the kitchen on top of the refrigerator.

"Lieutenant, whose responsibility is this?"

"Mine ma'am, but I assigned it to the corpsman."

"Don't you realize how many germs can fester up there? Didn't you check behind him?"

"I was busy with patients. He's an adult, ma'am. When I assign somebody a job I expect it will be done."

"So do I. See that it is. And in the future be sure that you follow up on assignments."

"Yes ma'am. Is there anybody coming into the VIP suite, Colonel Pecora?"

"Oh, I think they sent her to another hospital. At least your ward is spic n' span."

I respond with a nod and a smile, wondering if all this was one of her tricks.

In mid-April of 1965 I arrive at work, as usual, on the day shift to find a memo: "Report to Lt. Col. Pecora's office at 0900. "

Oh boy, what can this be about?   Surely she hasn't taken up this dust crusade again.   This place is at least 100 years old and certainly not airtight.   It occurs to me that I may be sent somewhere; but, I brush it aside.   It's too soon for that to happen.   Two hours fly by as I do reports and pass medicines to patients. In a rush, I leave the ward to appear outside the Chief Nurse's office on the dot of 0900. Hearing her business-like tone behind the door evokes a quivering in my gut.   With a nod, her secretary indicates for me to enter to meet my fate.

"At ease, Lieutenant."

"Thank you, Colonel."

"Read this and see if you have any questions." she says, sliding a paper across her pristine desk.

"2nd Lieutenant Patricia K. Brantley on standby beginning 0800Hrs., 15 April '65 until further notice. USAH, Ft. McPherson, Georgia."

Silence hangs in the room like the stillness before a tornado.   Then cold reality crashes in and the eye of the storm swirls in my head. This calls for stand-by, though, not a definite move out.

Maybe this is just a bad dream.   It could be a preview only of things to come.   Are they preparing for a war?   Who is doing this?

❧

*On April 30, 1965, the President of the
Dominican Republic is removed from office.
Government rule is seized by a new military
junta and call goes out for American support.
President Johnson responds by sending 1000
Marines and 2500 men from the 82nd
Airborne Division to the Caribbean island.
Their presence and support help prevent
Communist takeover and protect Americans.*

❧

Somehow I exit the Chief's office and stumble
down the hall.   Nauseous, I stop in the
restroom before calling Jim.   I can only
imagine his concerned expression as I relate
the news.

"Because I live within driving distance, I don't
have to remain within the confines of Ft.
McPherson." I say to his question.   He
promises to try to get home early.   How will
I ever get through this day?

"This means you have to stand ready to move
out in 24 hours," explains Sgt. Malick as he
reads the orders.   "I hear some have already
left for the Dominican Republic."

His grapevine is usually correct.

"What general area is that," I ask, hoping not to appear too ignorant.

"Well, let's just say it's not your usual Caribbean cruise, though you'll be in that vicinity.

∽ॐॐ

Later in the evening, while Jim and I are polishing off our butter pecan ice cream, we decide that the time has arrived to throw caution to the wind and the pills in the trash can.   Now is the time to begin our family, regardless of our financial circumstances.

Even if I conceive tonight, when the due date arrives about one half of my debt to the Army will be paid.   Do "they" care about me personally, anyway, and about the possible pregnancy?

After several weeks of living on edge, the word comes down, again via printed orders, that the alert status lifts as of 25 May65.   I put in a request for a two-week leave and decide to take a driving trip meandering down one coast of Florida and up the other side.

On Key West and other beaches, we revel in our togetherness, appreciating it even more because of our brush with separation. We don't speak of any further possibilities; though we know the threat is there.

"How was your trip, Lt. Brantley?"

"Fine, Sgt. Malick.   We needed the rest. Did you take good care of things while I was gone?"

"Sure, ma'am, with the help of the nurses." He chuckles.

We each fall back into the routines of our work.   No signs appear that cause us to suspect pregnancy.   Every month that passes we are disappointed.   Should we be tested for conception problems?   How long do we give it?   How much is too much?   We take my temperature and follow the "planned directions at the peak time.   You would think a doctor and a nurse would know what to do to make it happen.   We try abstinence and non-abstinence.   Nothing works.

The autumn leaves change to their golden and crimson hues and with them comes changes in our family.   My mother and her husband receive word from a friend that a baby, due in October, will be available for adoption.

It will be through a lawyer in Columbus, Georgia, the place of birth. Are they interested? They had applied through state agencies, but received no results due to age restrictions. Mother always wanted more children and my stepfather had never had any of his own. They both are thrilled at the prospect.

A trip to Columbus and a visit to the lawyer's office sets the process in motion. We know very little about the birth mother but we await the arrival as if she were one of our own.

"Why can't this be our baby we're expecting," I sob into Jim's arms one night.

"Aw honey, it will be one day. Just be happy for your mom and W. T. right now." He responds with an extra-firm hug.

"Oh, I am, but isn't it ironic that we're trying so hard to have one and here's someone giving one away, for whatever reason?"

"Yeah, too bad adoption won't work for us. I'm afraid the Army wouldn't buy that."

October 28, 1965, 9:30P.M., the phone rings at my parents' home. A nurse from the hospital in Columbus informs my Mother that her baby girl is born and is healthy.

They make plans to drive the 98 miles to see her in the nursery in the morning. When they arrive they are greeted with the news that they cannot see her, yet, due to the need for some further tests. Baffled, they contact the lawyer even though it's Saturday. He assures them that he will check into it and call them back.

They are staying at my aunt's house in Phenix City, Alabama, across the river from Columbus. He also calls the pediatrician. They meet at the hospital to clear up the confusion. They are reassured the baby is okay and that they can see her that same afternoon. She will be released on Monday. At that time, a third party must receive her without my parents' being present. My aunt, Mother's sister, assumes this role. My stepfather has to be at work on Monday so he can't be there.

The day arrives with anticipation. My aunt leaves Mother at a nearby grocery store to wait while she goes into the hospital. According to my aunt, the nurse wheels the birth mother, tears streaming down her face, into the hospital lobby. She passes the newborn, with care, to my aunt, who is crying, too. She snuggles her into a blanket. Without a word, the baby's future changes.

Nancy Anita Appling, five days old, nestles into the arms of her new mom, who cries tears of joy, as she and my aunt drive away to begin her new life.

We ride up to see her the night of her arrival. She brings renewed enthusiasm to all of us balancing the monotony of our work-pace and schedule changes.

Those nights when Jim's duty requires him to spend it at the hospital I stay in Marietta, visiting and playing with Nancy.

"For unto you a child is born.   Unto you a child is given."

The familiar words ring close to our hearts this year.   The holidays hold special meaning for all of us.   We continue to pray.

∽∂∾

Shortly after the toll of the New Year, 1966, another summons brings me to the Chief Nurse's office: "Report to Lt. Col. Pecora's office a 0900Hrs."

Here we go again. Nothing good comes out of these meetings.   What can it be this time?

Sitting across from her at the same pristine desk, I wince as she slides a paper toward me. As my eyes move from line to line I feel the blood leave my face like a bathtub drain, my ears buzz, as though a million bees swarm there, my eyes blur as if a drape of tulle drops over them like a veil.

"Lieutenant Brantley, are you alright?"

In the early days of 1965, the Viet Cong attack the U. S. base at Pleiku.   Eight Americans are killed leading to air raids on North Vietnam and escalation of the war in a skirmish named Operation Flaming Dart. Then the V. C. attack another base and Flaming Dart II is ordered by President Johnson.   In the weeks following this, Operation Rolling Thunder begins with continuous bombing of North Vietnam by the United States.

In early March of 1965, the first U. S. combat troops land in South Vietnam to protect the airbase at Danang—two battalions of Marines. One month later, President Johnson calls for peace talks with Hanoi.   They refuse.

In June, Air Vice-Marshal Nguyen Cao Ky takes over as prime minister of the South Vietnamese military regime. For three days in November, the first major ground conflict occurs in the Ia Drang Valley. The American troops defeat the North Vietnamese units.

In an attempt to negotiate, President Johnson suspends bombing on December 25th. By this time, the U. S. troops number 200,000. Americans killed in combat are 636 and draft quotas stateside are doubled.

The Longest Trip

2nd Lieutenant Patricia K. Brantley, ID# 255-65-5412:   Report for duty at Travis Air Force Base, Oakland, California at 0200Hrs on 11 March 66.

In one of those snapshot, burned-into- your-memory moments I look back at Jim through a fog of tears.   I wave as I move through the gate on the last boarding call toward my flight to San Francisco.   During the weeks leading up to this moment we talked long into the night. Often crying.   I even tried to swap orders with an unmarried nurse, stationed at Ft. McPherson, who had volunteered to go in my place.   But no deal-- and still no pregnancy.

Travelling in full, dark-green, winter uniform down to pantyhose and black pumps, does not lend itself to comfort and relaxation.   I try to sleep, knowing this promises to be a long trip, wherever my destination.   A myriad of emotions—excitement, fear, sadness—swirl through my mind, preventing more than fitful naps.

After a safe landing in San Francisco we board a bus headed for Oakland and Travis Air Force Base.   The bus fills with quiet conversation pierced with nervous laughter.

I sit next to another nurse whose name is Kathy.   We chat with ease.   She seems knowledgeable about our destination because she has a boyfriend in Special Forces.

"The hot spot," she informs me "is South Vietnam.   We have several hours before our next flight leaves.   Do you want to get a room on base?   We can get a quick bite to eat at the Officers' Club then go back there for a nap.   It's about a 13- hour flight if we are headed to Southeast Asia."

Grateful for someone who seems to know her way around and not wanting to be alone I follow the plan.   The club roars with a capacity crowd; but, we manage to spot a table.   The hamburger and fries are tasty, the draft goes down easy.   I feel the tension across my shoulders melt away.

We still have about four hours until report-in time.   Kathy assures me that her travel alarm will wake her.   I snuggle beneath the soft, cool sheets and sleep overcomes me.

In a single movement I sit bolt-upright, snap on the lamp and look at the clock that reads two a.m.   My stomach flips and tightens.

"Kathy, wake up, my God, we've overslept! What can we do?   They'll court-martial us!"

"I don't think they'll go that far.   Let's just get over to the terminal as quick as we can," she says as she rolls out, stands and stretches.

No one seems to miss us at the ticket counter. The terminal buzzes with activity, a blur of greens and blues

"Our flight actually left at 0200?"

"Yes, but no problem, ma'am, we have flights out every hour.   We'll get you on the 0400 one—Ton Son Nhut Airbase, Saigon, South Vietnam.   There you go—all set."

With a stunned "thanks" and a wan smile I take my ticket and move away from the counter.   It's official.   It is in print.   A year in this foreign land looms ahead.   Kathy joins me, ticket in hand, as we find seats to wait out the hour.

"At least the M.P.'s haven't swooped down on us, yet," Kathy quips.

My sigh of relief spurts forth as a laugh followed by a wave of nausea.

It's not over.   Somebody may have us on an AWOL (absent without leave) list, already.

At the appointed time we herd our way onto the huge jet and soon discover that we are two of three females on this 13,000-mile trip. Other than the weird ratio, the flight seems normal.   We play cards, read, eat and sleep our way across the world.

We touch down to refuel in Guam and in the Philippines.   As soon as the pilot announces our approach into Ton Son Nhut, hush as quiet as a cemetery at midnight falls over the plane. On touchdown, a spontaneous cheer arises, celebrating our successful landing.   But a thought haunts me—who among us will be on the return flight a year from now?

"Hi ladies, we've been expecting you," calls out a tall, well-built Lt. Colonel, as he jumps out of his Jeep onto the tarmac, as we walk away from the plane.   "I'm the C.O. (commanding officer) of the 36th Evac. Ready to go join your group?"   He throws our bags on the back of his vehicle.

◈◈

The last day of January, 1966, the U. S. resumes bombing of North Vietnam.   Peace negotiations have failed to take effect.

In the cities of Hue and Danang, Buddhist monks of demonstrate against the Saigon government in early March.   Government troops invade both cities.

In response to this, the U. S. bombs oil depots near Haiphong and Hanoi.   The North Vietnamese continue to infiltrate the South, aiding and abetting the Vietcong.

MACV Headquarters announces that they are using chemical defoliants to destroy the enemy's cover, which had been developed for that purpose.

On October 25, 1966, a peace plan comes after a conference composed of President Johnson and heads of six allied nations with involvement in Vietnam.   Those are South Vietnam, Australia, South Korea, New Zealand, the Philippines and Thailand.   They call for the end of North Vietnamese aggression.   By the end of 1966, the U. S. troop census in Vietnam nears 400,000.

The Caribou slows as it approaches the airstrip, hesitates, then descends further. Thump, roar, thud, rough touchdown.   We hold onto our seats as if they can save us. The plane rolls, then creaks and screeches to a stop.

"This is it, ladies, your home away from home," the pilot announces. "See those quonset huts across the tarmac? That's your quarters until your BOQ is built in town, six miles down the road—the big metropolis of Vung Tau."

There are 35 nurses in our unit, eight of whom are male. Since our hospital is not yet in operation, they were sent to the 93rd Evacuation Hospital, northeast of Saigon. When our hospital is activated they will join us.

Throwing her duffel on a cot, Kathy announces, "At least one of the huts has showers and flushing toilets. Are we lucky, or what?"

"Yeah, I can hardly wait to use 'em," I say, dragging my trunk to the side of the cot next to Kathy's.

"Can't you just feel that wonderful warm water washing this dust and dirt away?"

A fine layer of sand rests on every possible surface. Every time a chopper or plane takes off or lands, the particles fly around like bits of confetti during the Macy's parade in New York City.

"Come on, grab your towel," yells Kathy. "Let's check it out before we go into town for dinner."

Back from dinner at the Pacific Hotel, we find a notice on the hut door that reads, "Meeting at 1000 hrs., Lt. Col. Honeycutt's office. All nurses must attend."

Dear Jim,

Well, here we are after 18 hours of travel. We rode in a Jeep from the airport to the nurses' villa on the compound of the Third Field Hospital. How nice it was to stretch out even if it was on an Army cot with a thin mattress that sunk down in the middle. I'm sitting on one of them now, wearing my olive-drab fatigues and black combat boots.

Oh, yes, we were looking forward to a hot shower last night, but when I jumped in, all that was left was a dribble. Is that called a spit bath?

We'll be going by plane this afternoon to our "home" in Vung Tau, about 35 miles southeast of Saigon. The weather is sweltering, worse than July in Georgia. We will be issued jungle fatigues, lighter weight, which should help by a degree or two. Wish they could be shorts!

This is the strangest feeling to think that we are worlds apart.   While it's 0930 here, it's the middle of the night there.   On the way over, it was daylight the entire time, as if we were travelling backward, then, we crossed the international dateline and suddenly, it was the next day.   Was I coming or going? Anyway, I know I miss you, already.   This will be the longest year of our lives.

Please assure Mother that I'm safe and that I'll write more later.   We are going on a tour of Saigon and to the PX before leaving for our final destination.

All my love,

Patsy

In the Beginning

March 15, 1966.   We are the first American nurses in Vung Tau.   Everyone stares at us wherever we go, especially the soldiers, who are happy to see "roundeyes."

 In the "policy" meeting this morning, the Chief Nurse gives us a lesson in water conservation when bathing in a war zone: "You turn on the shower, step in, wet your body, then turn off the shower.   Using your washcloth and soap, lather and scrub your entire body.   Also, apply your shampoo at this time.   Turn the water back on and rinse quickly.   This same procedure, turning the water on and off, applies while brushing your teeth.   The water trucks don't run until tomorrow."

We exchange sheepish looks, vowing to try to be more aware.

Later that evening we settle onto our cots. Some girls write letters, some listen to music and some discuss our arrival.   The darkness falls over the airstrip area like a huge shadow of a beast hovering over its prey.

"What was that?" asks Della.   "I just saw a flash that looked like lightening.

She and Susan move to the door. "There goes another one sailing across the airstrip," says Susan.

"Turn off the lights and move away from the door.   You make a good target.   Those are mortars.   They can kill you." orders Esther in a loud whisper.

"Did you see that one?   It was closer.   What should we do?" shrieks Kathy.

"Shhh! Just drop to the floor," I answer from my crouched position beside the metal cot.

We watch the brilliant flashes illumine the night.   The flares arc over the airstrip and disappear into the inkwell of darkness. Thoughts of July fourth, falling stars, celebrations at home flood my mind as we huddle inside the quonset hut.   We are frozen to the floor in 100-degree weather, clutching our helmets like life rafts.

"Welcome to Vietnam! What in the hell are we doing here?" blurts Kathy.

I ignore her, hoping she shuts up.   We just arrived in this remote town this afternoon. Snatches of the brief welcome meeting with the Chief ring in my ears.

"We're very lucky to be assigned to Vung Tau. Its location, nestled in the lush Delta region, makes this one of the safest places for our staff and hospital.   Situated on the South China Sea makes it ideal as one of the in-country R&R (rest and relaxation) areas."

Her words reverberate, even as my brain is screaming.

No one prepared us for this.   How long can this last?   Where's our protection?

The mortar attack is over in 30 minutes. None of us sleep well that night.   The joke that circulates in the mess hall at breakfast is that the Vietcong knew about our arrival and wanted to give us an air show.   A definite baptism by their fire power.

I do not include this in my letter home.

Dear Jim,

Happy St. Patrick's Day!   We're having green beer tonight after dinner to celebrate. Wish you were here; or better yet, that I was there.   Hope things aren't too rough for you in the Pit (Grady emergency room).   How many hours are you on call and how many off?

*We went to the beach yesterday. It is beautiful.
The Chief advises us to expose ourselves
gradually to the sun because it's so brutal.
We only stayed two hours which usually is
nothing for me.*

*The Vietnamese women are very petite.
They're fascinated by us and by our size.   To
them, we look like Amazons.   They say that
we are, 'beaucoup kilos' meaning 'many
pounds.'   I will tolerate no comment from
you.*

*Anyway, they sell fresh pineapples on the
beach like ice cream cones.   The girl stands
there with her knife, holds the fruit by the stem,
peels it all around, cuts out the eyes and
leaves the stem on for a handle.   The charge
is 10 piasters, about 25 cents.*

*This afternoon we go tour the hospital
compound and meet the medical corpsmen
assigned to our units.   You can depend on
them to get the job done right.   Did I mention
that we are transported everywhere in three-
quarter ton covered trucks with wooden
benches along each side to sit on?   Maybe
I'll bounce some of this fat off if I don't get
prolapsed bladder and kidneys first.*

*Am anxious to hear from you.   I think letters
take five days each way.   Miss you and love
you.*

Always, Your Wife

⚬⌘⚭

"What?   Wh-what?"   I respond in a fog while trying to focus on the figure standing beside my bed.

"Pat, Lieutenant Brantley, wake up," she says, leaning over to touch my shoulder.   With a gentle shake she calls my name again, "Pat, Pat wake up."

I sit straight up in bed, now alert and awake. At this early hour the sun streams in around the closed curtains.   Maybe I'm dreaming.

"Would, would you repeat that for me, please, Colonel?"   I recognize the Chief Nurse, now, in the dim room.

"Your mother is in the hospital.   She had a heart attack on Friday.   That's all the message we have from the Red Cross. Signed by your Dad."

"Not my mother—you must have the wrong person.   My mother's never had any heart trouble," I respond, incredulous at this news

The Chief sits on the side of the bed, her hand on mine, in this strange room, 13,000 miles across the ocean, where Polly and I are sleeping after coming off night duty.

"How—how did you find me here?" I ask, a bit embarrassed at being in this pilot's room. When Polly presented the plan that morning it had sounded like a good idea—air-conditioning and privacy. She assured me that her friend was out on a mission and had offered his room in town.

"Some of the nurses remembered hearing you say that you and Polly were coming here to sleep," she replies. "We have arranged a flight for you to Saigon. It leaves from the airstrip in an hour; so, you need to ride back to the hootch with me to get some things together."

"You're sending me home? This is unbelievable," I mumble, dazed from the message.

Snatching on my fatigues and boots I look around to double-check for any loose articles.

"We'll be thinking about you. Be careful," Polly says, giving me a quick hug.

I move through the process like a robot. In Saigon, I only have to present the telegram, signed by my Father, sent through the Red Cross, to obtain priority for a flight home. In San Francisco, a stand-by flight to Atlanta requires just an hour's wait. People in uniform fly free on a space-available basis.

Within 24 hours I sit at Mother's bedside in St. Joseph's Hospital in Atlanta, Georgia. The oxygen tent's swish and the heart monitor's eerie glow combine to produce a surrealistic scene and knot in my gut.

My nursing experiences don't cushion the blow of seeing Mother as a patient, especially one in a life-threatening situation. My tears flow without control as the reality and gravity of the situation settles over me.

A Month to Remember

Within a week, the doctors announce that Mother has improved to the point that she can return home for continued convalescence. We assure him that someone is there to help her and the baby, at all times.   This month is when the final adoption hearing takes place in the Cobb County courthouse.   Nancy is six months old.

"I'm praying that this illness of your Mother's doesn't affect the adoption process," says Grandmother, voicing our underlying anxieties.

"Well, don't say that around Mother.   She needs to focus her energies on getting well, especially while I'm here to help with that."

"I know, she's had a lot on her lately."

"I'm going to try to get a hardship change in assignment, at least back to the States."

"Oh, that would work wonders.   We're all praying for that."

During the weeks that follow, we write letters, make phone calls, connect with friends and acquaintances. Maybe someone will know "somebody" who knows "somebody else" who might have influence to keep me from returning, at the end of May, to my duty assignment.

We all work at this at a frantic pace, knowing what my sentence is if we don't succeed. Surely, with my husband here and my mother ill, though no longer with her life threatened, someone can change those orders.

Jim and I spend as much time as possible with each other, working around his busy schedule on the emergency service at Grady.   We relish each moment; but, are always aware of the dark shadow that hovers over us.   We try not to talk about "when" and "if."   We reassure each other of our love and allegiance daily.

"What happens if you meet somebody else over there?"   Jim asks one night before we go to sleep.

"Nothing happens.   I'm married to you and I'm not open to anyone new."

"Yeah, but things happen when males and females are thrown together in different situations."

"I know.   Are you trying to tell me something?   I can ask you the same question."

"Your Mother and Grandmother keep me busy and well-fed," he says with a chuckle.

"Good, at least I know what you're doing some of the time."

"Well, that's just it.   Nobody's checking up on you!"

"You know you can trust me.   Besides, I'm a big girl now and can fight off the big bad wolf."

"Come over here and whisper that in my ear," he whispers, pulling me close.

ஒஒ

Mother continues to improve.   President Johnson focuses on troop build-up during this time.   Senator Richard B. Russell, our Georgia senator, chairs the Armed Services Committee.   The chance of any change in my orders looks bleak.   I'm doomed to return to the little village of Vung Tau, halfway around the earth.

Because my twenty-fifth birthday is on May 28th Mother plans an early celebration for me and for Nancy's final adoption.   It's a bittersweet gathering of family and friends. All efforts to obtain a "hardship change of assignment" have failed.   My leave ends May 27, 1966.

My real birthday starts at Travis Air Force Base while waiting for my plane to take off. Finally, at 0400, the big bird takes flight. There are lots of sailors on board going as far as the Philippines   About halfway there we fly over the dateline and suddenly it's tomorrow and my birthday is gone.

Before that, however, I pull out my piece of cake that Mother has packed and enjoy the memories.

I read; then sleep.   At 1600, I find myself rolling onto the strange yet familiar airstrip at Ton Son Nhut in Saigon.

Baptized by Fire

Stepping into 125-degree heat hits me in the face like a firewall.   I am back in-country. Someone from Vung Tau recognizes me and offers me a ride over to third ATCO where I can schedule a Caribou ride "home."   I wait for about an hour.

"Well hi, Lieutenant Brantley, what're ya doing here this late in the day?"

"I just got in from an emergency leave to the States.   I might ask the same about you, Lieutenant Lombardi."

"Oh, I had to make a quick run to pick up some supplies we need at the hospital.   I remember now.   It was your mother who had a heart attack, right?"

"Yes, but she's doing much better or I wouldn't be back.   How's everything at the 36th?   Have we been busy during this last month?"

Lt. Lombardi is the supply officer of the 36th Evac.   He fills me in on the news as we take the hour ride to Vung Tau.

When we arrive at the airstrip he calls an ambulance from the hospital to ride me to my hootch and him to the hospital.   Lucky for me that I ran into him.

After a brief reunion with some of the nurses, I take a quick shower and am out for the night.

In the morning sun streams in to awaken me. I'm not scheduled to work today so I roll over and go back to sleep.   I go over to Headquarters about noon and sign in from leave, collect my mail and chat.   Everyone seems concerned about Mother, which I appreciate.   The Pacific Hotel serves as the main officers' mess facility so I head into town for lunch.   This building also serves as quarters for some of the flight officers as well as the gathering place for movies and happy hour.

In the afternoon, I read some old newspapers then visit with Ruby and Jean who are off duty.   I write a letter to Jim.   I feel at loose ends trying to acclimate myself back into the "community."   Tonight, after dinner at the Pacific, several of us sit around the table talking.

"So Pat, what's the attitude back in the real world toward the conflict over here," asks Rudy, a Signal Corps engineer.

"There's lots of unrest and protest on the college campuses; but I didn't run into any open hostility myself."

"I'll bet you didn't advertise the fact of what you are doing nor wear your uniform unless you had to fly, or something," says Susan.

"No, but I came in contact with people who knew my situation and asked questions with genuine interest.   I didn't feel any hostility from them, though.   Some people really think we're doin' the right thing by being here."

"Well, we have to believe in 'the mission' for our patients' morale.   It's tough enough to get them well; only to know that they'll be sent back out to try it again," says Della.

"Listening to them talk, whether spoken or unspoken, you know they are feeling some of the same futility that we are.   I agree with you, Della. I do see being morale-boosters as part of our job as nurses," I reply.

The evening ends on a somber note, each of us lost in our own thoughts.   I catch a ride with Della and Bob, a pilot based here who has access to a Jeep   My schedule begins on the 0700 to 1500 shift tomorrow, Post-op Ward one.   While drifting off to sleep my thoughts turn back to home, wondering what everybody is doing tonight. Wish I could assure them of my safe arrival.

Back to work.   The pace has increased during my month away.   There are more wards open such as pre-op, post-op, numbers one, two, three and five, and a medical ward. Each one has a capacity for 50 patients.   The cots line each side of the quonset-hut walls.

Of the 41 patients on ward #1, 20 have shrapnel wounds, five have pungi-stick wounds (sharp-pointed sticks placed upward in a pit, covered with leaves, designed by the Viet Cong to maim, or kill, when stepped on), ten have malaria, an overflow from ward #5 and six have superficial fragment wounds at various sites.   Morning report puts names with faces and some of their stories.

PFC Rippey, frag wound of the left lower leg: continue the soaks and change the packing q4h," reads Lt. Maddox, the nurse coming off night duty.   "He had a pretty good night. He only had his pain med once.   Since this is your first day back, Lt. Brantley, the corpsman will show you how we've been doing the treatment."   She continues to hit the highlights, not naming every patient like we do in a regular hospital report with a smaller census.

We do the narcotic count and she signs off.   I feel a little insecure, but try to begin my rounds with a confident manner.

I approach each patient's bedside to introduce myself.   As we talk about each problem, I am struck by the young age.   I begin to look at each birthday as I flip through the cardex. Almost all of them are younger than I am! How can they face these life-threatening situations every day?

As I move from bed to bed, making eye contact with each man, I'm awed at the depth of their bravery.   By the time I finish making my way around the ward it's time to set up medications.   My first day on official duty passes without complications.   It's my turn to give report.

"Hey, Patsy," calls Della, on our way to catch the truck after work.   "Some Australian doctors are touring the Vietnamese hospital this afternoon.   Ya wanna go along?"

"Sure.   Now?"

"They'll pick us up in front of our BOQ in about an hour."

"Okay.   Isn't it on the road we live on but a little farther from town?"

"Yeah, I think so," replies Della.   "Guess we'll know pretty soon.   I think Pat H. is going and also a couple of Aussie dentists."

Our tour of the facility leaves us in a mild state of shock. They have about 400 deliveries per month. The mothers and babies room together—in fact, bed together— with four or five other mothers and babies in the same room. They stay seven days because some live 50 to 100 kilometers from the hospital and many have to walk that distance back home.

Most of the time, when the patient is admitted the whole family stays with them to cook meals for all of them. But the director, a Vietnamese M. D., studied in Paris for seven years, speaks fluent French and fair English, knows more progressive situations exist.

"...Happy Birthday to you. Happy Birthday, dear Buddha. Happy Birthday to you."

We sing a soft chorus of the familiar tune on our way to breakfast at the Pacific. I never knew that June third was Buddha's birthday. We pass under the "shrine" erected for the occasion, arching over the main road into town. His birth and death dates are B. C. and he died at the age of 80 years old. The arch is composed of blue brick-shaped material, trimmed with lights and brightly colored Buddhist symbols. The only evidence of celebration is that more people mill around like it's a holiday

"Let's celebrate by going out to the beach this afternoon," calls Cindy. "It'll probably be safer with lots of people out there."

"I'll catch up with you after work and we'll ride out together," I answer, jumping off the truck.

Since Vung Tau is designated as one of the R&R centers, the Armed Forces Recreational Services provides boats and skis, tables, chairs and umbrellas for those on leave and for those of us lucky enough to "live" here. We revel in the breeze as the Jeep whizzes by the rice paddies on the way to back beach. Cindy and I, along with a couple of other nurses, catch a ride with one of the pilots.

"What a picture perfect day," remarks Cindy as she throws her head back and lifts her face to drink in the sunshine.

"If you didn't know where you are you might like it," says Jean, a tall lanky blonde from Michigan.

There are two lifeguards on duty so one of them takes Cindy and me skiing double for a couple of rounds. I imagine that I'm at Cypress Gardens while I wave to people on shore.

"Did you ever think you'd waterski in the South China Sea?" Cindy asks as we lie sprawled on our towels while recovering from our exertion.

"No, seems like a dream here, but a nightmare in other parts.   This helps keeps your sanity when everything seems crazy around you."   I try to ignore the pull I feel in the backs of my legs.   My first trip to the beach since arriving back in country may prove how much I need to return to an exercise routine.

◈◈

Dear Jim,

This place is really getting to me.   Today depressed all of us associated with Ruby, one of our nurses who's a good friend of mine.   I think that I've mentioned to you in an earlier letter that her husband, Cliff, is over here with the "big red one" (first infantry division).

Anyway, Cliff was transferred to the 36th, to my ward, this afternoon while I was on 3-11. He was hit last night by shrapnel in the upper left arm.

Fortunately, there's no bone, nerve nor artery injury.   He was treated at the 3rd Surgical Hospital near Bien Hoa and transferred down here at his request.   The hole in his arm looks like someone threw a jagged rock and hit its target.

You probably know (from Grady) that these wounds are left open, covered with a sterile dressing then, after seven days, sutured closed. It's called delayed primary closure (DPC). The chance for infection is decreased greatly with this method. He says that he was lucky though, the guy right next to him, his radio operator got the top of his head blown off. If I were Ruby, I couldn't stand the thought of you out there in constant danger.

We heard this afternoon that a truck carrying soldiers and two or three doctors was riding through Qui Nhon, up north of Saigon. Someone lobbed a grenade in the truck from somewhere and they couldn't get it out of there fast enough. All of them are gone—killed. What a waste. It makes me sick to my very core.

Last night, two patients on my ward got into a fight. I suspected liquor was smuggled in and they had been drinking, but we couldn't find it so couldn't prove it. The corpman broke it up and no one was hurt. I had to call the AOD (administrative officer of the day) and write a report. Looks like they'd have enough fighting in the field.

About 2245 last night the ambulance brought in a sargeant DOA, who had been shot in one of the bars downtown. His rotation date back to the States was in five days.

They arrested two Vietnamese soldiers for it.
The "powers that be" in the Vietnamese Army
will shoot them as punishment.

I wonder about who's expecting that sargeant
back in five days. I'm going to take your
advice and not go into the town area after
dark at all. I can't imagine being here eight
more months.

There's only one empty bed on my ward
tonight. Those transfers from the 85th Evac
really filled us up. More about them later.

Received a birth announcement from Kathy S.
yesterday. She had a baby boy, 8lbs, 7oz, 21
inches long. Can't imagine my old nursing
school roomie with a baby. His name is
Christopher Allen and his birthday is June
14th. Maybe it'll be us next year.

Will close for now. Thanks for letting me
spout off. Give yourself a kiss for me.

Sweet dreams,

Patsy

Today is moving day, for sure. After so
many false starts and stops we move from the
quonset huts beside the airstrip into town to
the Army-Navy Hotel.

Kathy and I decided long ago to remain roommates, since we were so good for each other in San Francisco. By the time I got out to the huts after work, everything was moved.

Our room is an oasis with our own bathroom. The toilet sits on a small platform with a pull-chain flusher with a tank about two feet up the wall. French influence, I guess. A shower nests in one corner. We think it's the Ritz. There are men living on the first and second floors, most of whom hold MACV (Military Assistance Command, Vietnam) positions for Americans in Vietnam. We're located four blocks from the main market square which gives us easy access.

After dinner and the movie "Dear Heart" at the Pacific, Jim Hull, a pilot, escorts Susan and me home in a horse-drawn cart, one local mode of transportation. No one needs rocking to sleep tonight.

There's a Catholic girls' school across the street from our new villa. The buildings are yellow cement arranged around a courtyard in the center.

Looking out from our small balcony I watch the students in their white flowing aoi-dais and conical hats chatting and giggling on their way to school. Some walk. Some ride bicycles.

How much like children in America they seem, yet worlds away in this war-torn country. Their spirits seem to still run high. I wonder what their futures hold? Are their dads at war too? Maybe our presence here now can improve what's in store for them.

There are no certainties. I continue to watch until they are in class and all is quiet.

Anxious to take a walk after working the day shift, Della, Susan and I start toward town to New York Tailors. Della wants a silver bar sewn on her cap and Susan wants to pick up her tailored fatigues. Both of them were promoted to first lieutenant the week before. We have an hour to wait for the cap so we walk around to Cyrano's to have dinner. Jim Hull spots us and approaches our table.

"Do you ladies mind if I join you? Since it's getting dark you may want a ride to the villa."

"Sure, that'd be great," Susan speaks up.

 After dinner, Hull walks with us to the tailor shop.

"Get down! Get off the streets. Go back to post or to your BOQ (bachelor officers' quarters). There's going to be a war down here," the MP's come by shouting as we step out of the tailor shop.

"What should we do? Where can we go?" yells Susan.

"Look, he's motioning us to come back inside." says Della, scurrying back through the door held open by the small Vietnamese man.

We follow close behind her. No sooner than we step inside than two shots ring out about a half block away.

"Okay, go now. Get off the streets before somebody catches one of these stray bullets," the M.P.s yell again.

We hurry around the corner to the Pacific Hotel. Hull offers to go get a Jeep, take us to the villa. But an M.P. comes and we grab a ride.

They say that a bunch of Vietnamese Rangers started fighting with some G.I.s. Some of the G.I.s got cut, but none got shot. None of us has much to say to each other as we climb the stairs to our second floor rooms.

As much as I detest the night shift, I am thankful to sleep in this morning before going on at eleven tonight. Cliff, Ruby's husband, remains on our ward. His temperature spiked to 104 last night; so, they sponged him with tepid water to bring it down. I hope he doesn't have malaria. We all are supposed to take a "horse-size pill" every day to prevent it. There's a bowl of them in the mess hall as a reminder. Not everyone does this because it can cause upset stomach and diarrhea.

That night another patient spiked a temp of 104.2 and we only brought it down to 103 degrees after sponging.

"Ho Chi Minh's curse" finally caught up with me too. My head feels about ten times its normal size and I'm trotting to the toilet every 30 minutes this morning. The time in between, I am dozing and feeling terrible. During report this a.m. I went to the latrine twice to heave since that was all that was left in me. I took two Lomotils and two aspirin and am beginning to feel like I might live. I want my mommy and some chicken noodle soup.

In spite of my lingering queasiness I report in for the night shift. While making rounds and giving backrubs I am drawn into conversation with a blonde, blue-eyed 20-year old private first class.

"How'd ya get your leg wound, Private Johnson?"

"Well, I'm an r.t.o., radio transmitting operator, so I have to follow the platoon leader around. We were crossing a flat, open field area and I got hit in the back of the leg. My radio got hit several times before I did. I knew it was just a matter of time. I feel lucky to be here."

"You are. I'm glad you made it here, too."

"You know what bothers me the most is the hatred I feel—so much that I'm able to kill these people that I don't even know."

It's hard to respond to this.   I put my hand on his arm in an attempt to comfort him.

"I don't like to feel like that.   I—I hope when I get home all this hate will go away."

"War brings out the worst feelings in people. It helps to talk about it, get it out of yourself. You're in a situation where you have to kill to survive.   It won't be like that at home."   I sit a few more minutes with him, each of us lost in our own thoughts.   I squeeze his hand and move on to the next patient.

The rest of the night moves like a caterpillar inching its way across a garden wall.

At first light, we begin passing medications and getting everyone ready for breakfast. Those who are ambulatory go to the mess hall, wearing their blue pajamas.

Since it's Sunday I'll go grab a shower and a nap before coming back out to church and communion.   Susan and I usually sing in the choir, but I'm too sleepy and she isn't here. I will need all the spiritual strength that I can store up in order to finish out the year.

In the afternoon, the nine nurses and one medical corps officer who were promoted, throw a huge promotion party at back beach. There's a new snack bar pavilion across from the R&R beach.   The food is set up there. What a great spread, with chicken, bacon-wrapped fillets, baked potatoes and relishes. All the comforts of home.   We grill our own and eat under the pavilion.   Susan, Hull, and I had ridden the used bikes we bought; so, we are more than ready for food.

Some of the doctors organize a softball game. We opt to lounge and watch, saving our energy for the ride back to town.   This seems like such a normal scene.   It's hard to believe there's a war going on.   This is "Any Beach, U.S.A.

Since Sue and I are off until tonight, we decide to go around town with our movie cameras to record some local color.   We arrive early because the market closes by noon while everyone rests for a couple of hours during the hottest part of the day.

The children are my favorite subjects.   They are dressed exactly like miniature adults—silk pajamas or ao-dais (a female dress split to the waist with pants underneath) and conical straw hats.   Babies and infants wear shirts and no bottoms.

Some of them run and hide from the camera. We try to coax them with smiles and let them look into the lens. Mostly, they are shy and afraid.   Next time we will bring treats. Maybe they will remember us.

They seem like such a friendly, naïve people until I go to work and see their capacity for cruelty to our guys.   The maiming and killing from the mining, the shooting, the sticking, the blowing up, leaves indelible marks and scars on the psyche as well as the body. Mine as well as the patients'.

We have only twenty patients on the ward tonight so I can spend more time with each one.

"How're ya doing tonight, Applewhite?"   I ask, knowing that he had the delayed primary closure on his wound done today.

"I'm feeling pretty good for the shape I'm in. You know, I really wanted to get out of this armpit of a place before this happened to me. But now, I want to go back out and fight.   I couldn't stand being home knowing my buddies were over here fighting."

"Yeah, I see what you mean.   How do you tell the good guys from the bad?   I can't see any difference around here."

"It's hard.   We go on these 'search and destroy' missions and sometimes we don't know what or who to blow up."

He pauses for a moment. He looks distant.

"One time we found these caves, about forty feet underground, that contained radios, a communications set-up and medical supplies. These tunnels were dug that deep by men. Almost everyone has a tunnel entrance under his bed as an escape mechanism or hide-out."

"Wow—how do they survive?"

"Well, it's another world under there. They drink coconut milk, cook corn-on-the-cob in their steel pots (helmets) and eat bananas and pineapple. It reminds me of termites burrowing underground. We couldn't believe it."

We watch a t.v. that PFC Applewhite bought at the PX. The reception is fair, considering where we are located. We gather around it like a new toy on Christmas morning, even though none of the programming looks familiar.

Real ice cream and cake and cold Cokes greet us when we come into the lobby of the BOQ after work. Maybe Santa really did come today. Lt. Darla Waleska is celebrating her 23rd birthday. What a nice surprise for all of us. Earlier in the evening, my ward received thirteen transfers from the 93rd Evacuation Hospital. This is a welcome oasis.

Being near the beach and water-skiing becomes my salvation. Since none of us brought bathing suits to a war zone, we shopped for them in the market. What a joke! Finding large sizes proves difficult since all of the Vietnamese are so small.

Almost every day I feel compelled to make the short trip to the sea, either by bike, Lambretta (a small golf-cart-type vehicle) or hitching a ride. I have never seen bluer skies, whiter sands, or more inviting water. Or, maybe I'm just homesick.

One of the highlights on the beach is purchasing small, fresh pineapples from one of the many young Vietnamese girls selling them for 25 piasters each. When we finish this luscious treat our tongues tingle and sting from the acid. By the next time, we forget about the discomfort and repeat the process.

Tonight the ward is unusually quiet. The shift supervisor comes around about 2000 to ask the nurse, who is working with me, to go to another ward.

"Lt. Brantley, I need Lt. Brissell to go over and stay with one of our own nurses on the post-op ward. She was brought in earlier this evening with psychotic behavior, possibly due to alcohol intake."

"Sure, not much going on here. Is this just a passing problem with her?"

"Hard to say—seems she has numerous personal problems, drinking being only one of 'em. Hope we don't have to ship 'er out. Could be another casualty of war. We will evaluate her later."

While giving backrubs on my rounds, PFC Applewhite asks if he can talk to me when I finish. In about an hour I return to his cot.

"What's on ya' mind, Applewhite?"

"Oh, lotsa things. I guess I'm just thinking about going back out in the field. I want to go, like I told you before. But I might not be so lucky next time."

He leans his head back on the pillow and closes his eyes. Who knows what scene marches behind his eyelids?

When he opens them again the large, brown circles pool with tears and his pain is palpable.

I lay my hand on his arm.

"You wanna talk about it?" I ask.

Sometimes I feel guilty when I'm with the patients and hear their stories. My time here is so much easier than theirs; but our jobs are different.

After a long pause, he begins.

"They have a lotta tricks. When we're guarding the compound at night, the V.C. will throw rocks and you can't tell whether or not it's a grenade. The men duck into holes and nothing goes off—duck into holes and nothing goes off. And the very one that you don't duck for is the grenade.

"One night we went out on a mission," he continues. "It was so pitch dark that we had to 'lace' our legs together while we were lying on the ground. That's how we knew the other guy was there."

"That's gotta be scary," I said. "Even though you have guns you can't see your target."

"Thanks for listening, Lieutenant."

"Any time, Applewhite. Hope you sleep better tonight. I'll see you tomorrow night."

The ambulance driver forgot to pick-up the night shift, so we were late getting "home."

Moving day—again--third time in four months. We hope that we're at our final destination. This villa was built especially for the 36th Evac, but was late being completed. The building is similar to the one we just left.

I no sooner get my stuff piled in the room than it's time to get ready for work on the evening shift. Kathy, my roommate, has a shock in store when she gets in from work. She'll have to shuffle through piles of baggage to identify her things, though the movers did get most of the nurses' stuff up to second floor before leaving it.

Slept in this morning since it's my day off. It's much quieter in this location because the building sits back off the road more and there's less traffic on this street. I miss watching the school children, though-- a touch of home.

We still can walk to the Pacific Hotel and the main market place. Sue, Della and I decide to go shopping since they are off also. We find some paintings on raw silk and pillows that we like. We end up at Cyrano's for Cokes. Jim, the pilot, likes to hang around Sue so he joins our table. We all agree that it's been a good day even though it wasn't Rich's in Atlanta!

"Good Lord, Kathy, what was that?" I grab my helmet, roll out of bed and hit the floor in one motion.

"I don't know. What time is it?"

"0600—does it matter if we're about to die?"

All is quiet; then chaos erupts in the hallway. Everyone pours out of their rooms and we start talking and asking questions as the Chief Nurse comes up the stairs.

"Everything's alright," she says, stretching her arms and hands out in a calming gesture. "A hot water heater exploded on the first floor. It left a huge hole in the wall but no one was hurt. We believe it was an accident. You can go back to bed or get ready for work, ladies. By the way, there's no hot water for now."

"I'm glad we're on day shift since we're already up," I grumble to Kathy.

"Do you really believe that it was an accident?" She answers with a raised eyebrow and sharp look.

We find out later in the week that, indeed, it had been a grenade that exploded. The man who threw it was caught. A deserter from the Viernamese Army. He probably will be executed.

Dear Jim,

This has been one of the most rewarding days that I've spent in-country. I went on a mission sponsored by the Navy called Medical Civil Action Program (MEDCAP).

A volunteer group of medical personnel goes every Sunday by boat, called a sampan or junk, to a village in the Delta. They conduct a clinic to do whatever is needed for the natives who come. Our dentist goes every week and stays busy.

Anyway, Kathy and I, along with three other nurses, two doctors and our dentist went today. Word of our arrival spread and the people streamed to where we set up outside.

People presented with a variety of symptoms. Some had obvious vitamin deficiencies. We gave them vitamins. Some had infections. We administered Gantricin or Tetracycline. My job consisted of washing children who were covered in sores, with plain ol' soap and water. Then I applied Nitrofuracin ointment. It's amazing how much could be prevented with regular good hygiene. The dentist pulled about 200 teeth that day. That's the best he could do for them.

The village was a quaint little fishing villa, Phouc Thien, with sandy "streets" and crude houses. There were huge black nets strung out to dry. The smell of fish hung in the air. The people stood in small groups staring with obvious curiosity. One of the Vietnamese junkies, or sailors, gave me his black beret in a friendly gesture that pleased me. He wanted me to wear it as an emblem of thanks.

I wished for you to be there with me. We'd have made a good team. Remember when we talked about joining the Peace Corps? You would have enjoyed it, too...

Sweet Dreams

Patsy

Upon arrival in Vietnam each member of the United States Armed Forces receives a small card containing the following information:

NINE RULES: For personnel of U.S. Military Assistance Command, Vietnam

The Vietnamese have paid a heavy price in suffering for their long fight against the communists. We military men are in Vietnam now because their government has asked us to help its soldiers and people in winning their struggle. The Viet Cong will attempt to turn the Vietnamese people against you. You can defeat them at every turn by the strength, understanding and generosity you display with the people.

Here are nine simple rules:

1. Remember we are guests here. We make no demands and seek no special treatment.

2.   Join with the people!   Understand their life, use pleasant phrases from their language and honor their customs and laws.

3.   Treat women with politeness and respect.

4.   Make personal friends among the soldiers and common people.

5.   Always give the Vietnamese the right of way.

6.   Be alert to security and ready to react with your military skill.

7.   Don't attract attention by loud, rude or unusual behavior.

8.   Avoid separating yourself from the people by a display of wealth or privilege.

9.   Above all else you are members of the U.S. Military Forces on a difficult mission, responsible for all your official and personal activities.   Reflect honor upon yourself and the United States of America.

They are good rules to live by, but I wonder why it stops with nine.   No one ever refers to the card beyond including it in our packets of information.

Choir practice becomes a part of my weekly routine on Wednesday nights.   If I am on evening shift, and not too busy, I go the several steps over to the chapel for a 30-45-minute practice.

One of the guys plays a small pump-organ as our accompaniment.   It gives us a sense of normalcy, except for our olive-drab "choir robes."

On more than one Sunday morning, the nurses are asked to report to our respective wards, as casualties are expected at any moment.   We hear the "blap, blap, blap" of the choppers coming in and know that it's not a false alarm. It also brings us back to the fact that this is not a normal situation.   It's a war zone and we're in it.   We move at a walk-run pace to await the "cargo" being off-loaded at the chopper pad, marked with a huge red cross.   We hope some of our morning prayers are answered as we wait in anticipation, dreading the unknown.

I am sleeping with a "Dutch husband" now, thanks to a trip to the Vung Tau market, after work today.   This "husband" is a long cylinder-shaped pillow that's a great bed fellow.

We also bought baskets that I'm using for clothes.   As a test, I asked my "mamasan" (person who cleans and washes) to buy one for me.   She paid half the price that I had. It's no wonder that they're glad we're here. Their economy will never be the same.

In Saigon, we see signs of American dress while we try to find "ao-dais" big enough for us to wear. This native outfit consists of pants underneath a flowing dress split up to the waist on both sides with a high mandarin collar and long sleeves. Most are made of satin with a brocade pattern. They look feminine whether the wearer is walking or riding a bike.

Lt. Colonel Hall, Chief Nurse, addressed the subject of shopping on the economy, warning us to be aware of prices and our money exchange. She reminded us that male visitors, including officers, to our rooms should be limited. She also informed us that a trip to Bangkok, Thailand on the C-140 counts as a three-day pass, not as annual leave. We all applauded that announcement. Della and Sue are scheduled to go tomorrow. I hope I can go soon.

Since I have no annual leave left, due to my trip home and the trip to Hawaii, this will be a good way to see another country. Over dinner tonight Della and I talk to several of the pilots from the 61st Aviation Company about the Bangkok trip.

Only two or three nurses can be gone at a time. You leave on a Friday morning from the Vung Tau airstrip and return on Sunday afternoon.

The Century Hotel is where everyone stays, so you are not out there on your own.   Sounds like I can squeeze in some sightseeing and shopping even in that short period of time. We will know more details once the others go and return.

LT. PATRICIA BRANTLEY

*Author as student nurse (top) and in Army
Nurse Corps uniform (bottom)*

Vietnam Women's Memorial, Washington D.C.

Scenic view of a Vietnamese coastline

The author (center) and her mother Juanita Appling (2nd from right) with recruiters on swearing-in day

Author (left) at her Army Nurse Corps induction

Patient beds in Quonset hut hospital ward

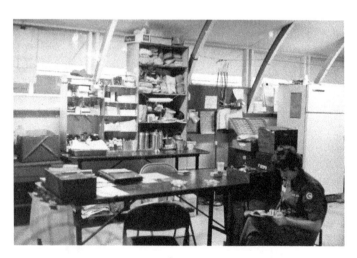

Nurse's station at the 36th Evacuation hospital

*Patient out getting fresh air (top);
"Mamasan," cleaning woman for hospital
(bottom)*

Prepping pineapples for market (top)

Street scene in Vung Tau, Vietnam (bottom)

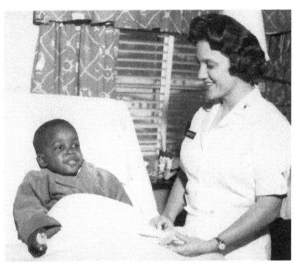

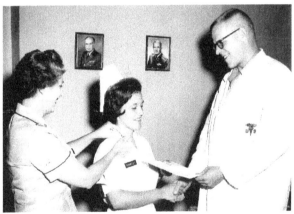

Author attending to a young patient (top) and being promoted to 1ˢᵗ Lieutenant (bottom) at US Army Hospital, Fort McPherson GA

Dr. and Mrs. James W. Brantley on their
wedding day

Routine Always Changes

July 22, 1966: "Lt. Brantley, you're not gonna believe who's coming to our ward today."

As I approach the desk to begin the day-shift report I am greeted by Sergeant James, the ward master.

"Try me. I'm all ears."

"General Westmoreland, himself!"

"You're kidding. What'd we do to deserve this?"

"Seems he's dropping in this morning to give some purple hearts and talk to the men."

Sure enough at about eleven, there's a small commotion as the door to the ward opens and in strides the General, "Westy," followed by his entourage. We all come to attention.

After greeting us and ordering "at ease," he stops at each one of the twenty-two cots, asks each patient's name, unit and circumstance of his wound. He awards several purple hearts and signs the certificates. One patient, Staff Sergeant Charles Neal is recommended for the Congressional Medal of Honor.

"From what I know about him, he seems like a great guy to me, General."

"Very good, congratulations, Sergeant."

"Thank you, sir."

We move down the line of cots to for his exceptional bravery under fire. The general converses with him about his experiences.   I offer him a congratulatory handshake.

"Do you think Sergeant Neal, here, is a good soldier, Lieutenant Brantley?"

Private First Class Riley, who was lifted out of the combat zone where he was wounded, hanging by a quarter-inch rope attached to a helicopter.   He was suspended this way for a ten-minute ride because there was no place clear enough for the chopper to land.

General Westmoreland's party consists of his new aide, Captain Frank Carpenter, formerly the "Lonesome End" on the West Point football, team and a photographer with "Life" magazine.   The story goes that while in the field Captain Carpenter called a napalm attack in his own area because his unit was surrounded by the Viet Cong and there was no other way out.

My body knows when it's Saturday. Kathy and I both overslept this morning. We were late for the day shift truck. The hospital administrator sent the Colonel's car to pick us up about 0745. There were no repercussions as the census is low.

My ward master built some shelves for our room out of scrap wood. He heard me say that we needed some in our bathroom at the hootch and one to hold my tape recorder. He surprised me with two sets. We 'll take them "home" on the truck at the end of the day.

Sue and I ride into the market on our bicycles to pick up the curtain that I had made for the front of the shelves from a roll of thin pink plastic. A soft rain begins so we stay in the shop until it stops. The lady who owns it has three children who are playing around the counter with plastic toy guns. Her baby looks about six months old. She breastfeeds while we're there. Some things are universal. What do their futures hold?

Early the next morning, on my day off, another nurse, Claire, and I rise early, eat breakfast at the thirty-ninth Signal Battalion quarters, hitch a ride out to the airfield, catch a ride on a Caribou plane to spend the day in Saigon. I feel a little fear mixed with my excitement; but Claire has done this before and assures me that we'll be fine. How does she know?

Our first stop is the huge Post Exchange. It's much better stocked than the smaller one in Vung Tau. Two hours seem like thirty minutes. For a few piasters (Vietnamese money) we take a ride into town on a Lambretta, similar to a golf cart; where, at The Continental Hotel, top floor, we enjoy a wonderful American lunch.

After lunch, we stroll down Tudo Street, the Rodeo Drive of Saigon, enter a few shops but find that most of the local clothing is too small for us. In spite of crowds milling about, we "round-eyes" attract stares and occasional whistles, more from the Americans than the locals. By fifteen hundred we board a Lambretta and return to the airfield. We don't want to miss the last flight back to Vung Tau before dark.

The flight crew does the usual checks while we board the aircraft. We settle onto our bench-type seats. As the plane revs up, the noise prohibits normal conversation so I lean my head back and close my eyes. It's been a long day, but a good one. I'm looking forward to using the new reel-to-reel tape recorder that I purchased. Our return flight seems short as I drift into sleep, waking with a start when we touch down at the Vung Tau airstrip. This is the same one where we arrived many months ago. Or was it years? I keep reminding myself that this is one of the "safest" places to be—if we have to be here at all.

Since this town is one of the in-country R&R centers, the U.S. government keeps the beach area in top condition. Activities are provided by the recreational services division, such as a couple of motor boats for skiing and fishing, so that G.I.s experience a relaxing three-day visit. Lifeguards have posts on the beach in certain areas also. "The Beachcomber," a snack bar pavilion, across the main, provides the usual grill and snack menu for a small fee.

On this particular day, Sue and I take refuge from the sudden downpour that occurs often and without warning. Our cheap bikes can use a shower while we sip our Cokes and enjoy the view.

We fall into a comfortable silence.   Since
Sue hails from Florida and I from Georgia,
this feels as close to home as it gets.

Dear Jim,

*Hi Love, what were we doing at this time three
years ago?   Remember all the excitement
and fun we had getting ready for our wedding?
I want to be with you right now.   Will time
ever pass? I miss you so much.   This better
be the only anniversary that we spend away
from each other.*

*One of our patients bought a T.V. at the P.X.
We watched "Bewitched" the other night.   It
was frustrating, though, because the picture
and sound would disappear for a couple of
minutes; then, nothing but snow on the screen.*

*Anyway, I was thinking that if I could just
wiggle my nose on the 28th that we could
actually be together for a celebration!   How
does that sound?*

*Renae and her husband, Cliff, are staying in
the guest room here.   We should be so lucky.
He's well from his wound and is on pass now.
Not so lucky that he will be returning to duty
soon.   I hope this thing is over when it's time
for you to do your service.*

Changes occur every day in the hospital.
We've opened another medical ward and set
up additional beds in the other two wards.
About four hundred beds is capacity. Thank
God they're not all full. After the recent
bombings in Hanoi, our post was put on alert
in case of retaliation. So far, all is quiet on
the western, er, southeastern front. We are on
extra alert, yes, but how safe are we, really?

It's pouring rain right now. Sure wish I was
home in bed with you. I'm mailing a little
package for you. No, it's not me.

Sweet dreams, Sweetheart.

O O X X X X

Happy third anniversary: July 28, 1966. I
celebrate by riding to the beach with Sue on
our bikes. The lifeguard offers to take us
skiing. We'll get some extra exercise as well
as sore muscles. Our time is cut short to
hurry back and catch the truck for the evening
shift.

As soon as report finishes and the shift leaves
I notice a huddle around a bed near the ward's
back door. Thinking they are playing cards,
I begin setting up the medicine tray before
making rounds.

In a few minutes, I catch a shuffling movement in my peripheral vision. Turning toward the noise, I am greeted by eight smiling faces as the group marches toward me.

"Cheers and happy anniversary, Lieutenant Brantley!" They sing out in unison as they lift a bottle of champagne.

"Someone pop the cork," pipes up Lieutenant Cook, whose injury doesn't allow him out of bed.

Since the patient census numbers below fifteen everyone enjoys a medicine cupful before the bottle runs dry. My checkers-playing buddy, Chief Warrant Officer Ralph Holloway, claims responsibility for the surprise, as he proudly presents me with my own bottle for celebrating after work. He suffers a shrapnel wound in his lower left leg from flying a mission in a Huey helicopter down in the Delta region.

Strange how the smallest things seem hilarious after splitting a bottle of champagne. Throwing Della's stuffed bear, "Killer," off the balcony of our BOQ tonight sends us into gales of laughter. When I go to rescue him, attempting to "fly" him back up, he lands in a puddle of water, while four other girls act as cheerleaders.

"HAP—PEEE ANNIVERSARY!"

It's taking a while for me to get moving this morning. My head feels too heavy for my body. Thank goodness for the 3 to 11 shift again. Susan and I meet in the mess hall for supper and decide that we should continue our celebration tonight since it's actually July 28th in the States. Jim should be celebrating today. It's only logical that we should, too.

Fortunately, French champagne is on special at the Pacific Hotel tonight. Sue buys a bottle. Our plans for splitting it after work change, however, when several girls show up to help us drink it.

Wonder if they heard about our party last night? I'm sure we'll be glad in the morning. Goodnight, Jim. With my forever love.

We change to the night shift (2300 to 0700) tonight which gives us a long day before reporting tonight. The 39th Signal Battalion BOQ has its own chef who never minds our eating there. He probably likes the "round-eyes" and we like the cheeseburgers. We head to the market after exchanging some money to piasters. Kathy buys a bamboo curtain for our bathroom door and some fruit for herself. There are differing opinions on its safety. I hope it doesn't make her sick. I pick up a painting of my sister Nancy that I had done from a photograph. It's a pretty close likeness. I think Mom will like it for Christmas.

The census on the ward tonight is low.   All
remains quiet until I'm called over to cover
Ward Two, next door, for part of the night.
The nurse there is admitted to Post-op with
"Ho Chi Minh's Revenge--" nausea, vomiting
and diarrhea.   I am empathetic, but hope the
germs aren't flying around her ward.

Attending chapel on Sunday morning, held in
the mess hall on the hospital compound, gives
some structure to our lives.   We ride out on
the quarter-ton truck so no spiked heels today.
I sing in the choir because I like it (not
because I can sing).   I like to attend choir
practice on Wednesday night when schedule
permits.   My friend, another nurse, plays the
small pump organ, like one we had at church
camp.   The choir director flies Caribou
planes during the day.

  We decide to have Sunday lunch at a local
restaurant that has proven to be safe.   I order
shrimp thermidor and Sue orders fried shrimp.
We drink iced tea, pretending we are sitting
on Peachtree Street back in Atlanta.   The
streets begin to clear as people go inside for
naps during the hottest part of the day.

Back at the BOQ I discover that Della has the
afternoon off as we do.   It's a perfect beach
day; so, we ride our bikes out for the exercise.
Lucky for us, the boat is on the water and we
get invited to ski. "You like?   You like?"
The young Vietnamese girl approaches,
carrying a basket of small, fresh pineapples.

"How much?" I ask her.

"Uh, fi-p, fi-p," she answers.

I pull out five piasters, nodding my head to indicate "yes." She wields her knife, holding the pineapple by the stem, begins to peel and carve the fruit with deft hands. I'm under her spell again. Maybe it will not make my tongue sore this time.

In less than a minute, she extends her offering toward me, flashing a wide grin. From my first bite into that golden, succulent flesh I'm hooked. By the last bite, my tongue feels raw from the acid, but it's worth every bite. Will I ever learn?

Each one of us copes with the stress of being here in different ways. What works for some of us doesn't work for others.

We found out more information on the nurse, female, first lieutenant, about thirty-three years old, was admitted to our hospital last night with psychotic behavior. She has been in the Army for a year, is divorced and has a history of numerous personal problems.

The post-op ward has a corner screened off and reserved for any female patients. It offers little privacy, however. That is why the charge nurse pulled the nurse on duty with me this evening to go sit with the new patient because she has to be restrained. She continues to fall out of bed.

No one seems to know what action will be taken in her case. There is some talk of sending her to the Third Field Hospital in Saigon for treatment and recuperation.

How could anyone find solace anywhere here if you're already bombarded by constant fear? The "powers that be" will no doubt find a way to return her to duty before sending her stateside.

The word came down yesterday that we are receiving a group of transfers from the 93rd Evacuation Hospital at Long Binh, above Saigon. Most of them are ambulatory, according to the chief nurse. Some still need a DPC (delayed primary closure).

Another group of patients who have come to our ward recently are Australians. They have started an operation near here so their wounded are treated at our hospital. Most of them have great personalities, funny and love talking to Americans. Their accent is tricky to understand.

As well as doing wound care, lately we have had a run of patients spiking fevers-104-104.3. This requires sponging the patient with tepid water to bring the fever down as quickly as possible.

Each one has to have lab request slips written for malaria smears to be drawn at the time of the fever. The diagnosis is determined by searching for parasites in the blood sample.

According to Ivan L. Bennett, Jr., in Principles of Internal Medicine, "malaria is a protozoan disease transmitted to man by the bite of Anopheles mosquitoes...it is characterized be rigors, fever, splenomegaly (enlarged spleen), anemia and a chronic, relapsing course."

Even though the occurrence of the disease has declined since 1945 due to an active international program of malaria control, the influx of human hosts in this part of Asia has caused renewed exacerbation of the disease.

With the prevalence of rice paddies, drainage ditches and dense jungle growth the opportunities for breeding are plentiful.

We are expected to partake daily from the bowl of orange anti-malarial pills placed at the end of the chow line in the officers' mess hall, the Pacific Hotel.   It is tempting to skip the pill because of the possible side effect of diarrhea.   It's our choice.

The timing of the dose is important because if you have to ride the truck out to the hospital and the side effect kicks in, it can get uncomfortable.

The scenario of the guy with chills, then fever, then sweating flashes in my mind.   The temptation to skip the dose passes as quickly as a mosquito bites.   Then I feel the urge to grab a handful.

I don't remember my dad nor my uncles mentioning this as part of the World War II daily regimen.

Moving through the chow line at the Pacific I take a seat with some nurses at a large table near the center of the room.

"Well, I see you've got 'cha big orange on ya' tray," says Paula.

"Yeah, thought I'd try not to go home with anything extra, including VD.-ha.   Don't know about my sanity, though, it's taken a few hits."

"I know what 'cha mean.   We had an influx of sponging to do on the medical ward last night.   Almost everybody decided to spike at the same—omigod—what was that?"

"V-ROOM!   KA-BOOM!"   Silence.

We all freeze.   Looking at each other, wondering when and where the next explosion might occur, or whether we should take cover before it hits, we try to resume our normal posture.

"Sounds like a grenade," says Sue.

"No, it was too loud for a grenade.   Had to be something bigger," says Todd, one of the nurses.

We don't get the straight story until the next morning when I report for work.

It was a claymore mine that was planted by a tree beside one of the bom-de-bom, or Ba Muoi Ba beer stands.

These stands along front beach, downtown, about two blocks from the Pacific, are just little open-air wooden sheds where the GIs sit around and drink "33" beer. It's a Vietnamese beer under French license that packs a powerful wallop, according to the guys on my ward. I've only had a sip because it tasted funny and I don't like beer anyway.

No one knows what triggered the plant. Ten GIs were injured and one killed. The three worst ones were the one with his foot blown off and the two who lost an eye. Another one suffered a serious abdominal wound. The surgeons operated almost all night. We admitted three to our ward and the rest are on the post-op ward.

This proves once again that there are no "front lines" in this war. No one knows when nor where Charlie, dressed in his black pajamas and conical-shaped hat, will hit. We have to use good judgment; but it is impossibly stressful to constantly live on the edge of fear.

We had a V.I.P. visit our hospital this evening. After eating supper in the mess hall, Arthur Godfrey, with his flaming red hair, freckles and ukelele toured every ward. He visited with the patients, sang and told jokes. He definitely lifted everyone's spirits. Toward the end of our shift, word came around that any nurses who are off in the morning are invited to the beach with Mr. Godfrey. The Special Services carry-all will pick us up.

"Come on ya'll, he's here," yells Paula, standing in the hall of the second floor BOQ, "your chariot awaits."

Sure enough, peeking out my balcony door, I see the van with Mr. Godfrey waiting inside. I grab my cover-up and bag and fly down the stairs. I don't want to get left behind. We bump out the road to the beach with light conversation flowing. He wants to know where we're from and how we got here.

"I've been wondering that myself," I respond.

He throws back his red head and lets out a big belly-laugh. "You girls are a breath of fresh air in this war zone. No wonder the guys want to keep hanging around."

We spend the morning swimming and chatting. Since he had a successful radio show for several years he's a great conversationalist, putting all of us at ease.

Each one of us tells our story of her journey to this place. Each one is unique and each one has its purpose. He actively listens with rapt attention.

The highs and lows of this place can be compared to that of a psychiatric patient's manic depressive syndrome. The night shift is miserable wherever you are pulling it. We have eight patients tonight and four of those are being discharged later this morning. My little radio plays low, the corpsman lies on one of the empty cots and I sit here trying to stay awake by writing a letter to Jim while being "in charge." Maybe I can take myself back to the beach if I close my eyes; but, then I might go to sleep. Only four more nights of this torture before I go back on the evening shift, my favorite.

Food becomes one of the great rewards for ourselves. Kathy and I bought three baguettes (must have learned from the French) in the market the other day. They were delicious with peanut butter from the PX and peach jam from C-rations that Susan found. Oh so gourmet, oui?

Canned food (C-rations) is what the troops eat in the field. They come twelve units per case. Each unit contains a packet with salt, pepper, napkin, plastic spoon and three cans. One can has meat, one the "dessert."

Here are the choices for dessert. You could get fruit, cake, crackers, or a small roll of white bread and a small, flat can of peanut butter, cheese spread, or jam.

The meat choices are boned chicken, ham slices, dehydrated ham and eggs, chicken and noodles and beef and potatoes. They are tasty, but better if heated. Some weeks, canned sodas are available in the PX.

Our "mamasan" brings us ice for 20 piasters. We keep it in a small ice bucket that we bought. It's funny how important a cold Coke can become. I miss having ice cream more than any other food. We can eat at the 39th Signal Corps mess hall for seven dollars a month. They serve big, juicy hamburgers at lunch and wonderful french toast for breakfast. Their BOQ, located around the corner from ours, is closer than the Pacific. Sometimes they show movies after supper on the open-air balcony that serves as their bar. It's nice to sip a gin and tonic while watching a shoot'em up cowboy movie.

Although the administration discourages it, we eat "on the economy," at local restaurants. There are a few known to be "safe," sanitarily and militarily. We don't go often nor take chances. It's best to mix it up and not establish a routine.

Cyrano's remains our favourite, since it has an outdoor patio overlooking the water. We can almost forget where we are.

Request for leave has to be submitted forty-five days prior to the date of departure. There can be four nurses away from the hospital at any given time, which is ten percent of hospital personnel.

Jim and I write each other constantly about the best time to meet in Hawaii. Of primary importance is planning the date around optimum time for conceiving. Another factor is when he can be away from his intern rotation at the Emory-Grady-VA Hospitals. All this needs to be coordinated so that hotel reservations and airline reservations can be made.

My official request is 28 October 66 to 08 November 66. The personnel officer, Lieutenant Cole, says that it has to go up through channels. It might take a month and a half to two months to be approved or denied. On leave, as opposed to R&R, I am responsible for my own transportation. If I cannot fly on space available, or standby, I'll have to pay for my own way which is about $500 round trip.

"If only I could call you and talk about it," I wrote Jim, "now we just have to wait and see."

We admitted another unusual patient yesterday. Her name is Toi and she's two years old. Her sister stuck her in the eye with a knife. The Aussies discovered her while on MEDCAP and brought her with them to this hospital.

Our eye surgeon operated and probably saved Toi's sight. She'll be on the post-op ward for about a month.

Though it's a sad case, she has added a new dimension to the patient care. Most of us have been by to meet her, probably our maternal instincts kicking into play. She is hardly bigger than a one year old.

One of our patients is named in a long article that appeared in the Stars and Stripes, the Army newspaper:

Aussie Unit Faces 100-to-1 Odds—and Wins.

The article names Private B.C. Mellon as one of the survivors. It relates his story close to the way that he told it to me.

"Mellon, wounded in the face, leg and shoulder and unconscious, later told of being jolted to consciousness by something tugging at his feet. He looked down to see two Viet Cong trying to remove his boots. Mellon shouted at the startled V. C., who turned and fled."

"Mellon then spotted a wounded Viet Cong reaching for his weapon. He crawled to the guy and killed him with the V.C.'s own weapon.

"When the relief troops arrived they found Mellon propped up under a tree, holding the V. C.'s weapons. 'I knew you'd be around, mates,' he told them."

There are ten patients on the ward at present. Rumor has it that the 173rd Airborne and the Marines started an operation yesterday, somewhere in this vicinity. Grapevine is usually correct. Everyone seems tense.

If we receive patients from the field, our duty hours may increase. It still amazes me how quickly the wounded bounce back to duty.

One patient transferred in from the 85th Evac will be going stateside as soon as he is able. He had an enucleation of the left eye due to an injury.

This is a nursing first for me. I have to remove his eye implant, wash it with soap and water, lubricate it with an antibiotic-based ointment and replace it. All my nursing school lessons are challenged, as well as my anxiety control level.

He remains stoic and brave while I am replacing it. He says that it feels like it is going up into his head.

Another patient transferred to us today will be hard to forget.   His injuries occurred when a land mine exploded under pressure.

According to his chart, he has an open fracture of the skull, right frontal bone, caved in due to a penetrating fragment wound.   He has a fracture of the left parietal bone due to the first injury.   He also has a laceration and contusion of the left frontal lobe of the brain due to that injury and a laceration of the right eye from the penetrating fragment wound, plus, multiple fragment wounds of the head, neck, chest, shoulders, arms and abdomen.

He comes to us in a normal neurological state after being comatose.   He needs his sutures removed from the delayed primary closures and follow-up care by the ophthalmologist and the neurologist.   Of course, he will be evacuated to CONUS, or continental United States.

He's only twenty years old.   When will it all end?   Do boys like him even know why we're here?

We rarely know ahead of schedule when an "important" visitor appears.   Fortunately, I'm working the day shift today when the two-star Commanding General of the First Infantry Division appears on our ward with his entourage.   He's come down to present his men with their combat awards.

There are twenty-one just on our ward. All of them receive purple hearts. In addition, there were two silver stars, two bronze stars with valor and one Army commendation medal. It's inspiring to see them recognize these heroes, pinning the awards right onto their blue pajamas.

This afternoon, one of the surgeons, Dr. Vinnie, gives a lecture to the nursing staff on "Amoebiasis," or, amoebic dysentery. We've had two or three cases of amoebic liver abscesses at the 36th. All of the guys were in-country for six months or longer, before noticing the symptoms of dysentery and griping pain caused by the amoeba which can lead to the erosion of the intestinal wall. Also, they all consistently ate on the economy. "Charity," the chief nurse, and her staff must think we need this lecture, too. That's enough to take your appetite.

Today is election eve and all is quiet around town. In fact, it is scary, as if a lion is about to pounce. You know he is lurking, but you hope he will not attack.

Banners for candidates are everywhere, written in Vietnamese, of course. Almost every house and building displays the yellow and red South Vietnamese flag, just as we do our own flags in the States. They do not want the northern sympathizers' candidate to be elected. Who knows what the future holds for them?

As a precaution, the 39th Signal guys send vehicles over to pick us up for supper since we cannot be on the streets. The fried chicken and ham remind me of my southern home.

As a special treat, there is a Philippine band with a female vocalist. The music lifts our spirits for a while, then the three-quarter ton truck transports us to our villa without incident. An armed guard stands at alert on the back of the truck with us like an escort.

Because the C120 cargo planes are stationed in Vung Tau and make frequent trips to Bangkok we can request a three-day pass for a week-end hop without taking annual leave.

My name has come up to go with another nurse for the coming week-end. The break will be a treat—hot baths, iced drinks, delicious food, sightseeing and shopping. All the stories I've heard are about to come true for me, too.

My feet finally land on Thai soil. Buddha is everywhere in Bangkok and it seems that every Buddha has its own opulent temple. Standing in front of the Emerald Buddha, surrounded by gold leaf and lacquered walls, I feel awe and a spiritual lift despite the strange environment.

From our base at the Century Hotel we go to the silk factory on Saturday. There are housed many of the beautiful handwoven fabrics. Then on to the jewellery stores we go, where we bargain and shop for presents. In the evening, a couple of the pilots take another nurse and me to a local Thai restaurant. The food is spicy and delicious— it's lucky for us the guys know what to order. There's also live music to make the evening special. Back at the hotel we enjoy a late-night swim in the pool and feel safe. Since we have to leave on Sunday, we have to try all the amenities.

The floating market happens only on the weekend in the early morning. Many of the people live on the riverbanks, so their "homes," or boats, become the marketplace. Food, as well as other products like plants and teakwood articles, bring droves of people out to shop. We decide to go by on the way to the airstrip, but don't have time to linger. It only whets our appetite to return for a longer visit.

The flight back to Viet Nam happens too fast. No one talks much. We know what is ahead of us.

"Y-i-i-i-Ha-a-a!   The half-way mark arrives—six months down and six to go. Another big X in the box signifies the halfway point as we check off this day on our wall calendar in our room.

There's a party in the villa to celebrate and several people have open houses in their rooms.   We make the rounds, raising toasts that our next six months will fly by and take us all home quickly and safely.

Dear Jim,

As of now, no word has come down on my request for R&R in Hawaii for November. There are lots of requests for it and enlisted men get approval before officers.   My time in country meets requirements so I should be ahead of others.   I know you have to get your ticket, too.   I'll let you know as soon as I know.   I miss you bunches.   What if we don't get to meet there?   It'll ruin our chance to make a little Melanie and cut my time here short.

This is my first night on the eleven-to-seven stint.   We only have fifteen patients on the ward tonight but there are two "boarders."

Friday evening, three Vietnamese, one woman and two men were brought in, wounded by a claymore mine. The woman has a baby about a year old, her husband is a Vietnamese soldier. He and the baby are here visiting her—our C.O. consented to let them spend the night with us.

I have all three of them on the ward. The baby has cried out several times, but the father quiets him. He even got up to get milk from the refrigerator. Will you do that when the time comes? And change diapers, too?

About a week ago, the C.O and the Ex. O. of the advisory team in Vung Tau approached Rachel and told her that two very nice Vietnamese girls were interested in meeting some American girls. They want to learn English, and about our culture.

They asked if she would be interested in meeting with them. Of course, she said yes, and asked me to help her organize some information.

On Friday, the Colonel picked us up at the villa and took us to the Vung Tau City Hall, where the girls work. They seemed so sweet and eager to learn. They already speak some English. I'm sure we will learn plenty from them, too.

They invited us to their house for dinner the next night. We accepted and really enjoyed it.

They served us rice with a choice of different sauces to top it, such as beef with dried bean sprouts, one made with shrimp and others. It was all good, that is, what I could stuff in my mouth while using chopsticks.

One of the girls' father is the veterinarian for the Vung Tau area, so her family is well-to-do compared to the majority. Our plans are to meet with them twice a week for classes. We're really looking forward to it and I'm sure they are too. They agreed to teach us some of their language and customs as well.

One of my best buddies, Sue, has about sixty days left. She gets out of the Army on Jan 1st--"fini," done. "They" say that if that is your final date then that you'll probably leave here in time to be home for Christmas.

She and Sharon both are due out then. Lucky, aren't they? Sharon is the nurse who's married to an Army enlisted man--lab technician in the States. Sue's planning to come to Atlanta to work, but hasn't decided where.

Well sweetie, this wraps up the news for now. Almost time for some shut-eye.

Oceans of love with a kiss on every wave...

The Long-awaited Aloha

Can this actually be happening? I'm on the "big freedom bird," as we call the plane taking us away from Viet Nam, to the great state of Hawaii. It feels like I am soaring to the heavens. The plane is loaded with people as excited as I am, though all but one other is male. Outside the window I see only blue skies as I look down on the tops of fluffy, white, cotton-ball clouds. In my mind's eye I see Jim flying from the opposite direction to converge at the same point on this island of paradise. Our planes actually do arrive within an hour of each other, with his being ahead of mine.

As we deplane, a grass-skirted wahine places a lei of fresh flowers over my head. "Aloha...aloha!" she and the other woman greeting us say.

The sweet aroma swirls around me as I walk toward the main terminal. Then I spot his eager face in the crowd, scanning the passengers, towering over the people in front of him.

Our eyes meet. A big grin covers his face. My arm flies up and I break into a sprint, in spite of heels and uniform.

Our bodies meet in a tight embrace—at last. If only this moment could last forever. It seems like time slows down.

We start laughing and talking at once, while emotions spill over into tears. On the ride into town I try to enjoy the scenery but I cannot look away from Jim for fear he will disappear. I keep touching him as proof that he's actually in the cab beside me. Finally, we arrive at our hotel and paradise begins.

Oahu emits an aura of Eden-lush, green foliage covers a large portion of the island. Water sparkles with sunbeams bouncing on the waves like fireflies at night. Surfers catch a big one now and then. Girls with flowing dark hair wear bright, swinging mumus. Deeply tanned guys sport colorful, casual shirts. Waikiki Beach looks shorter than it appears on "Hawaii Five-O;" but, I thrill to the picture of myself flying through the water on a surfboard "catching the wave." Instead we opt for a stroll to absorb the beauty around us. The weather is milder as well as several degrees cooler than Vietnam.

"Look at those moves. I want you to practice that dance for me tonight," whispers Jim.

"Maybe coming to this Kodak show was not such a good idea. Better snag one of those Tahitian dancers for some private lessons if you're expecting that from me."

"Oh, come on now, Pat, I'll buy you a grass skirt."

"It'll take more than a grass skirt for hips to move like that. They're amazing. Nobody's out of step and they're moving fifty miles an hour. Can you imagine how much practice that takes?"

More than a thousand years ago, Polynesian voyagers brought the spirit of aloha to the Hawaiian Islands. A melting pot of diverse cultures are exhibited during this show. The hula, which means "dancing" in Hawaiian, is our favorite because the dancer tells a story with her graceful arms and hips movements while swaying to the ukelele or steel guitar. Our program says that the word "ukelele" means "leaping flea." Not a pretty picture; but their dance is exquisite.

Shopping in Honolulu proves to be an exciting experience. An area set up as a Polynesian village sells products from the various areas— wooden articles made from the monkey pod tree, some shaped like pineapples and jewellery fashioned from the ginger flower blossoms or pod seeds.

I picture the prints of native flowers and woven designs hanging in our den.   Tent-like booths are filled with colorful mumus, aloha shirts and bathing suits.   Most clothes here hang loose depicting the casual lifestyle, but also catching whatever breezes float by.

Tiny bubbles—in the wine

Make me happy—make me feel fine.

Tiny bubbles make me warm all over.

With a feeling that I'm gonna love you

till the end of time.

Don Ho croons his smooth tune on stage in his club, where we go for dinner.   We sway to the rhythm and join in singing on the chorus. Then we break into the refrain from "Guantanamera," the hit by The Sandpipers.

The week has passed as if it were only a brief moment.   We are in another world, though the stars look the same.   As we gaze up at the night sky from the balcony of our hotel, I push away thoughts of my return trip and try to live in the moment.   At least for this evening, we avoid the subject.

As we ride through the crowded city on the way to the jet airline terminal we see hotel construction in progress, as well as a new state capitol being built.

Most of the growth, according to our cab driver, is taking place on the island of Oahu. He says there are plans for resort areas on the islands of Hawaii, Kauai, Maui and Molokai. The natives worry that as the tourist business increases it will become harder to preserve the natural beauty of the island.   A stir is brewing right now, he tells us, about building hotels and high-rise apartment buildings on the slopes of Diamond Head, the famous extinct volcano near Honolulu.

We're thankful for his running conversation. It is a temporary distraction from the impending doom of our flights and parting, like prisoners going to the hangman's noose.

After a deep, passionate kiss, I begin the endless walk to the big bird that will take me away—again.

I can't help turning to look back at him, waving until he becomes smaller and smaller. As I peer out the plane window I see him straining to find me.   I wave, but know he cannot see me.

Holidays and Hoorays

"Whoever heard of Thanksgiving in a mess hall?" complains Lucy.

"Just be glad we're in here and not sitting in the middle of the jungle, getting shot at while trying to eat turkey from a can," popped back Cindy.

For some of us it is the first time away from the comfort of family or friends during a holiday time.   We began the day with a service of Thanksgiving at the chapel on the hospital compound.

The choir sang to the music of a new, bigger organ which sounds better than the portable pump organ of before.   Since I attended choir practice last night, I joined in with them up front.

Then we proceeded to the 39th Signal Corps mess hall. We got turkey with all the trimmings, including a finale of pumpkin pie topped with whipped cream.

Our family of nurses tried to be brave while we speculate on what our stateside families may be doing. We traded stories of past celebrations and imagined where we might be this time next year.

The unspoken truth was that, like our patients, none of us really knew if we would be here the next day, much less the next year.   Of course, our chances were considerably better than soldiers we treated and sent back into combat.

We often wondered about the well-being of those we sent to various places, whether to a larger hospital in Saigon, back to their units, to Camp Zama in Japan, or to the States for longer recuperation.

Occasionally, some word came through, some in writing and some by word of mouth, such as this one from "R. R.."   He was a patient on our post-op ward for several weeks with multiple shrapnel wounds requiring delayed primary closures.   He could be up and around, so he had a chance to visit with other patients and staff—nice guy—good for morale.

Well, how is the "Southern Belle" of the 36th Evac?   I hope this finds you and the others in good health and fine spirits.

I understand there have been a few incidents in Vung Tau lately.   I guess the V.C. on R&R. there are getting restless.

As you might have known, we are now involved with "Charlie" up near the Cambodian border in Tay Nihn Province. We have been most lucky with no serious injuries so far.

I hope we shall return to base camp by the first of Dec. I've only got 64 days left in this place and do admit I'm getting homesick.

Well, I shall close for now. Just wanted to let you and the others know how much us guys thank you all for all that you do for us when we are there. You, yourselves, do more for our morale and physical being than all that medicine you stick us with at times. So thanks again for a job well done. Hope all of you have a most gracious Thanksgiving.

Love Always,

R. R.

About a week after that letter, a postcard arrived from a patient who was at Camp Zama, Japan:

Well Ma'am, how's everything in V.N.? I'm doing fine. Walking a little better now and chasing after the nurses that I can get close to. They have a fine hospital here but I don't like the staff as well as I did there.

I want to thank you for the fine treatment I received while I was there and on my behalf I'd like for you to thank the rest of the staff for me.   You are a fine bunch of people and are very much appreciated.   If you get a chance drop me a card.

Yours, LD

Their thoughts and well-wishes caused us all to marvel at how they could be thinking of us while they were in, and had experienced, far worse situations than we even could imagine. We wrote back, but did not hear again.

Right after Thanksgiving we receive a flyer:

DOUBLE DIGIT FIDGET PARTY

Fun   Games   Food Drinks

99 DAYS!!

Wednesday 30 November 1966

1900 hours

Second Floor Ballroom---Villa

Your Hosts...

This was followed by a long list of the hospital staff who came over on the original flight.   What a wake-up call.   Though we were among them, it's a shock to see on paper that we're officially known as short-timers, that is, less than 100 days till leaving Vietnam.

A popular topic of conversation during the evening of celebration was our stateside assignments. The general consensus was that surely after paying our dues over here, Uncle Sam will give us our first choices.

The count on the ward during December reaches its fifty-patient capacity and holds there for at least a week. The end of our shift comes quickly on days like this. We receive word that there may be some "activity" in the Delta vicinity soon, so some of our patients are scheduled for transfer to clear beds for future casualties. There are no definite orders at the end of today's shift.

"Do you want to go Christmas shopping this afternoon," asks Kathy, as we meet each other outside the ward. We fall into step on the way to the truck to catch our ride into town from the hospital compound.

"Sure, you wanna go to Rich's or Davison's?"

"Alright smarty, but we've got to have everything in the mail by December thirteenth to be there by Christmas."

"First, let's put up the little tree I brought from Hawaii to get us in the mood. I'll put on that Christmas tape I bought, too."

"Great, let's do it!"

With renewed energy, we chatter about our ideas for gifts, over the noise of the vehicle, while we bounce our way back to our villa.

By the time we arrive, we are eager to begin our project. Being off the next two days should give me a great start. With any luck, the PX has received their shipment of Christmas cards. This Christmas will never be like the "real world," but maybe we can make it as close as possible.

Today I received my "Christmas box" from Jim. All the wrappings look so pretty and festive. I had sent him shopping at Rich's for special charms for my close friends here. We decorated our door like a Christmas package, so we are never sure what's behind it when it's opened. Our friend, Rachel, made a tissue paper wreath for the finishing touch. We are playing the cassette tape of Christmas music as much as possible to keep "our spirits bright."

On our shopping trip for gifts to send home, Kathy and I bought beautiful raw silk for dresses, native-dressed dolls for my sister and nieces, tie tacks and elephant hide wallets for the men. We also found decorative and useful wooden items as well as delicate paintings on silk.

Along with work, our shopping, wrapping and mailing before the deadline of December 13th kept us almost as busy as being in the States during the holidays.

Our Christmas party in the hall, held on December 21st, lifts everyone's spirits while we decorate the tree, sing carols and open gifts.   We each brought a dollar gift which was distributed by "Santa Claus" (one of our more rotund doctors).   His suit was tailored in town, but his beard remains a mystery.

My special gift is a brown coffee mug with "Lt. Brantley" etched on it.   I can almost smell the coffee perking in my mama's kitchen. In my mind's eye I see our den, full of ribbons and wrappings, the eggnog flowing, the bantering and conversation filling the air.

Roommate Kathy left early this morning for R & R in Malaysia.   She and fiance, Felix, a tough Special Forces guy whom she met while stationed at Ft. Bragg, NC, arranged to meet there to try to get married.   She was giddy with excitement, so I look forward to the details when she returns.   The rest of us get back to "business as usual."

"There shall no evil befall thee, neither shall any plague come nigh thy dwelling.   For he shall give his angels charge over thee, to keep thee in all thy ways." (Psalm 91:10 & 11)

This verse, sent to me in a letter from my grandmother, runs like a reel in the back of my mind.

I do not feel fear all the time; but, whenever I hear distant shelling or see the devastation it brings, or even imagine the possibilities that could be, I try to re-roll that tape and recite that verse. Her voice plays in my head.

The post-Christmas week passes on a quiet note, almost as if 'Charlie,' in his fancy black pajamas, has taken his own vacation.   With the new year fast approaching, spirits seem lighter—1967--our year to return to the "real world" with "real people."   We feel the mood shift.

The special flyer promises festive food and live music at the New Year's Eve party planned at the Pacific Hotel.   The atmosphere buzzes with excitement on the second floor of the medical BOQ in anticipation.   Those who are lucky enough to be off duty scurry to be ready for our ride in the quarter-ton truck.

"Lucy, can I wear your yellow blouse tonight," yells Sue from across the hall.

"Sure, just don't spill nothin' on it," says Lucy.

"Do you have any of that *Toujours Moi* perfume left, Della?   I'd like to wear some since this is a special occasion and I'm wearing normal clothes."

Our group of nurses gathers downstairs, at the main door to await our ride, when a Jeep pulls up.

"Guess who's at the party tonight, ladies," announces Major Baxley, "none other than -- John Steinbeck!   We've come back to get our books for him to sign.   Just happen to have a couple of 'em with me."

"Wait for me.   I think I have *Travels with Charlie*," I yell, while running up two flights of steps.

The air of joviality in the Club, even though a war zone, is at high pitch.   The anticipation of a better year to come is palpable.   Moving through this rowdy crowd toward the opposite side of the large room proves to be a challenge. At last, there in black and white, the tape above the left pocket on the olive-drab jungle fatigues reads: STEINBECK.

His brown beard, his slightly curly, medium-length hair give the appearance that he might have lived in the jungle himself for a while. Observing him for a moment while he chats briefly, then signs books, I see a genuine warmth radiate his round face and clear blue eyes.

"And your name is--?"

"Pat," I reply, handing him my book.

"Have a seat, Pat."

"Sir?"

"Have a seat.   This chair is empty."

We chat with ease. He asks how it is being a nurse in a war zone. I ask him if he's there researching a new book. After a while, I move on to give others a chance to enjoy this rare privilege.

Even after stepping out of his aura, I cannot shake the feeling of awe at meeting someone whom I studied in school. You know he's one of the best, yet here he is thanking you for your service to our country. Catching snatches of conversation around the club I can hear Steinbeck's name rise with a voice, as word travels that he is here.

If only Jim were here too, so that we could be enjoying this together. I wonder where he is tonight, as I do every night; but this one seems more poignant.

While singing "Auld Lang Syne" and cheering in the New Year, our thoughts turn to home and better days ahead. We all hope that next year will find us in a different world.

Sat. Jan. 7, 1967

Dear Pat,

Grady is upon us. I'm busy again after being on Pathology and it's great. Doing lots of surgery. Wish I could have anticipated your coming home while on Pathology, though, so we could have had more time together.

Have you heard anything yet?   You should hear soon.

I got your tape about Christmas.   Glad you liked everything.   Again, my watch you gave me is great.

No, I'm not going to tape in a public place. To tell the truth I prefer letters to tapes especially since I'm not at the VA any longer.   By the way, write your mother.   She's worried due to no letters.

I spent New Year's home in Wrightsville but had no luck hunting.   Everyone's fine there.

It's lonesome around here. This letter seems dull and short but can think of no more to say except I love you.   Write!

Love, Jim

Soon after the turnover into 1967, on a Saturday right after lunch, our Chief Nurse calls to say that Kathy and I are expected the next day in Long Bien for an interview with Colonel Pixie, commander of the 68th Medical Group.   He will either approve or disapprove our promotions to Captain.   She suggests that we "brush-up" on current events, the history of the Army Nurse Corps and the history of the 36th Evac Hospital.   What?! How the heck could we do that in less than twenty-four hours?

These interviews are a new part of the Army Regulation that dropped the time-required length for promotion to Captain. We are the lucky first ones to go from our unit, so Lt. Col. Hall had no idea what to tell us about it. We pick up our orders from headquarters Saturday afternoon then wait, talk and sweat. Lt. Col. Dubois drops by our room that night just to talk. He reassures us that all will be well. I am sure he senses our apprehension.

A male lieutenant from the dispensary picks us up Sunday morning at 0630. We awoke to a dark stillness in the air. The generator is off so we dress by candlelight. Hope this is not a bad omen. Our plane, an Otter, a small eight-seater leaves at 0730. After a smooth ride we arrive in Bien Hoa. Someone calls the group headquarters and they send a Jeep for us, about a twenty-five minute drive from Long Bien, on a four-lane highway, no less, using the term loosely.

Our appointment is at 0900. We arrive about 0930 so the Colonel is waiting for us. Kathy dives in first, only stays a short while. Later, comparing notes, we find out he asked us both about the same things only based on our individual records.

"Lt. Brantley reporting as directed, sir," I say while saluting.

He shakes my hand, tells me to have a seat.

"How do you like the Army, Lieutenant?"

"Well I enjoy my work," I replied, trying to evade the question.

"Do you plan to stay in?"

"I haven't decided yet," I said.

We chatted about Georgia while he perused my records.

"Well, you have a good record. I'm going to recommend approval of your promotion. There's just one other question I want to ask you..."

Uh-oh. Here it comes.

"Do you have the feeling sometimes that the U.S. Is in over its head here?"

"Yessir, I do."

"Well, if you were the President," he said, "what would you do about it?"

"I'll tell you what I wouldn't do right now and that's get out. We've committed ourselves, come this far and to leave now would seem like such a wasted effort. I don't have a solution. I know it will take a long time to complete the mission."

"Yes, that's right," he said.

He shook my hand, thanked me for coming while I saluted and left.

❦

The 93rd Evacuation Hospital here at Long Bien seems quite drab compared to brighter and greener Vung Tau, located on a sea coast.

Hi Honey,

I'm coming home!!!!!

Would you believe 65days at the most?! It doesn't look very promising that I'll be leaving earlier, as we had hoped. I can't realize that I'm finally "getting short."

This is a number ten week. I'm on nights as of Tues. and am absolutely good for nothing. I've slept practically all day but still feel draggy.

Rachel is looking forward to the week-end off when she goes up above Saigon to visit her husband. They sleep in a tent for privacy when she goes. I have to work through Sat. night, if I survive, then back to days. Guess I'll have to settle for playing my Hawaiian tape and dream. It's pretty but it makes me lonesome.

Hope you remembered your sister's birthday today. It slipped up on me but am sending some Vietnamese lounging pajamas from here. Hope she'll like them.

Did I tell you the coincidence that happened when Kathy went to Malaysia? She left from Nha Trang so she stayed overnight there after leaving here. Her roommate was Marian Abner that good friend of mine at Ft. Sam, from Wisconsin. She came over with the 12th Evacuation Hospital. She said that she will try to visit us in Vung Tau before we leave—only 65 and a wake-up!

Our latest patients went to the Post-op ward, two Vietnamese women and two children with burns from one of the villages.

Well Love, will close for now. Don't work too hard. You have to be in good shape for when I get there (chuckle). M-m-m-m-SMACK,

love ya', Patsy

Packing crates and organizing shipments of personal goods consumes our time away from the normal shift at work. Although days are cooler, low eighties, we still spend some free time cycling to the beach, not really thinking we could be popped off at any moment. A hostile disturbance was rare in this sea coast town. We probably should wear a conical hat and a flowing ao-dai, then we would not be so obvious on our mode of travel. Days pass with a syncopated pace, some fast, others slow, as we tear each one off the calendar.

Here We Come World

Dear Pat,

Glad to get the good news about reassignment to Fort Mac.   That's at least one worry out of the way.   I don't like the sound of them talking about March though.   I surly have been hoping it would be sooner.

I have this week-end off and we have talked some of a fishing trip.   I'm not sure yet what'll come up but Panama City has been mentioned.   If anybody goes, and I'm not too tired tomorrow night, I may decide to go.

I still haven't heard from Sue.   Was she going to be here awhile or just passing through?   I talked to MaMa today and they are alright in Marietta.

This year at Grady is not quite as good as last year on General Surgery.   I do bigger operations but not as many.   We still have not had a patient with a gunshot wound. Guess you've seen some though.

I miss repairing hernias and such! I have to pass those down to my Jr. Residents.

Also, the patients I operate on are in really bad shape so they have long drawn-out post-op courses. I'd rather they were ready to go home in five to seven days.

Feeding Rip (the dog) is really a problem now since I'm gone about every other night. I never get to play with him so he probably feels as lonely as I do. If you didn't like him so much I would give him to a happier home.

The car is running bad. Needs a tune-up and new tires but none of that is under warranty so we'll have to pay for it out of pocket.

Well, I need to go downstairs and check some patients. Will close for now. Write.

Love,

Jim

It seems impossible that rotation back to the States can be only eight weeks away. I thought I would be here forever. The fact that the hospital received some transfers from the 93rd who were wounded the day before practically fills up my ward, therefore making time pass quicker.

In fact, the enlisted men go home next month because they, along with some of the administrative officers, left the States a month before us and came by boat, which takes about three weeks; but, they will be flying back to the real world.

It is difficult to believe that one can contract a common cold in this tropical area: drippy nose, watery eyes, hacky cough...

We are freezing over here.   It goes into the sixties at night and early morning, then up to the eighties around noon.   The natives are wearing sweaters.   We are wearing our fatigue shirtsleeves rolled down instead of up.

Dear Love,

We received some more transfers yesterday afternoon from the twelfth evac.   These guys were not as freshly wounded as the ones the other day.   So we had less wound care, soaks and dressings to do.

Well, they're giving us another C.O. And moving our favorite, Lt. Col.Dublin, up to the 93rd evac where our old C.O.   is and he goes home in Feb..   The new guy is here but we haven't met him yet.   We're having a farewell party for the Lt. Col. on Thursday night. That's my day off so I'll be able to go.   Then on Friday, I start back on nights.   Seems like I just got off that shift!

Glad you are getting some good operating experience. That would really be great if you could trade services then I could have you all to myself when I get home. Not much news here. Will write more later. 'Night, I love you so very much...

P

Sometimes the longing and need seems overwhelming. It's those times that I walk outside for some fresh air or sit in the gazebo that was erected on our compound for gatherings, and try to read. We seem to be in a time-warp.

Everything is surreal. My time at the beach has been a godsend for calming my restlessness. How long can a year be? Will it ever end? One good thing about this dormitory/communal living there is always someone willing to talk and to listen. Will I ever see or hear from some of these people again? What will it feel like if I do? Everything real seems so far away.

"Captain Brantley" has a nice ring to it, but I don't recognize the person being addressed. Kathy and I were finally promoted on January 28, 1967, in a little ceremony in the C.O.'s office Lt. Col. Cyprus pinned the cloth "railroad tracks" on our fatigues as one of his first duties at the 36th Evac.

My date of rank will be back-dated to November 1st; but, I will only receive pay beginning January 20th.   No questions asked, no answers given.

Some of the original staff who came over together almost a year ago are beginning to rotate back to the U.S. of A.   Our registrar left yesterday by ship because he has a fear of flying.   It takes about three weeks that way. We will miss his jolly face and laughter-- always upbeat.   Only about forty days left for us.   I'm trying to pass it by reading, taping music, sunning and, of course, working.

One of my many supporters during this span is my Grandmother B.   She sends me letters on a regular basis and seems to know when my spirits need lifting.   She gives a running commentary on the activities of my baby sister.

Nancy and I have been up since 7:30 since mother had to leave around that time.   Nancy played with her white shoes for a long time, the laces were out which made them more interesting.   Mother had washed them. Then she played with some cups-- stacking and unstacking.   Now she's into the magazines, looking at them...

This scene gives me a true picture of Nancy's personality and activities.

My grandmother never fails to include a short clip of a Bible-related reading which always seems to target a need.

For this particular day she encloses:

"Psalms 23:2. 'He leadeth me beside the still waters.' The shepherd well knows that, if his sheep were led to water beside a fast flowing turbulent stream, he would jeopardize their equilibrium and sense of balance and they would topple into the current. Their wool would fast become soaked and heavy, and the sheep would be carried downstream and lost.

In this turbulent, convulsive age of uncertainty, chaos, and despair, it is imperative that time be taken to bask in the presence of the Lord, in quiet repose....'beside the still waters,' to maintain our equilibrium, our true sense of values, our effectiveness as soul winners.

Not only shall his name be called 'Wonderful, Counsellor, The mighty God, the everlasting Father, Prince of Peace'...but 'the Lord is my SHEPHERD.' (author unknown)"

Am so thankful you will be home soon. Looking forward to seeing you and being with you. God bless you and bring you home safely to us is my prayer. Love you.

How well we know these are turbulent times.

Care packages have been regular treats during our long year.   Some consisted of simple needs such as hair bands, hair rollers, lotion and even candy and gum.   During the summer months one creative   friend put together a "picnic basket" full of supplies including peanut butter and jelly, chips, crackers, pickles and olives, paper plates, napkins and a red-checkered tablecloth.   We had fun with that at the beach.

Of course our Christmas packages were on schedule and all very special.   January did bring a late fruitcake, mailed in December but still tasty (well-aged).

In early February, however, one arrived by surprise because it was too early for Valentine and too late for Christmas. I tore into it expecting lots of red but instead faced an array of orange and black.

Turned out to be a Halloween party in a box containing all the ingredients for a spooky night of celebration!   Wonder what circuitous route it took since September? Considering the quirky arrival time, it was on a "slow boat to China," or in this case, to Vietnam.

During this last month in country we are busy measuring our possessions to have crates built for shipping them, deciding what to take and what to throw, packing clothing into suitcases. We are allowed sixty-six pounds on the plane but can ship six hundred pounds to arrive in about a month. All the while we continue to pull our shift. My ward remains almost at full capacity.

On one of my recent nights off we attended a USO show on the base and thrilled to the beat of "These Boots Are Made for Walking" belted out by the real Nancy Sinatra strutting her stuff in those knee-high white shiny boots! "And one of these days I'm gonna walk all over you..." Yahoo!!

A few days before our due date to "di-di mau" (leave) the country my mouth erupts with ulcers and I begin to run a fever. What can be happening to me after all this time with no major illness? Now I have this "plague" on me!

I feel horrible but am determined not to let anything hinder my departure. Surely this will get better and go away. I do not go to sick call right away even though I can only tolerate liquids, due to the pain.

Twenty-four hours before departure, I give up and go seek help.

With no time to grow cultures they attack my problem with a huge dose of bicillin. Now I am sore somewhere else, but hope my mouth begins to heal during the long trip on the "freedom bird." Much to my relief, they make no mention of delaying my flight out. I intend to be on it.

We sit in quiet anticipation prior to our last lift-off from Ton Son Nhut air base. Everyone seems deep in his own thoughts: hoping this is reality, mulling over the past year, willing the plane to take off before anything can happen to delay us.

As the wheels pull up into the underbelly of the plane and we feel the surge of the lift off the ground, a simultaneous cheer goes up, fills the air and tears of joy and relief fill my eyes.

Good-bye to the piles of sandbags, good-bye to the strange smells hanging in the oppressive air, good-bye to the niggling fear at the base of my brain, good-bye to the "thwap thwap" of the helicopters overhead, good-bye to Vietnam.

None of us can return the same as when we went over.

Loaded with aspirin for the pain, I sleep the majority of the flight until we land in the Philippines. When our plane finally touches down in California, another spontaneous cheer fills the air. It feels good to know that we are safely on U.S. soil.

We swarm into the terminal, head to the nearest ticket counter.

"When is the next flight to Atlanta?"

"What are the chances of getting a seat?"

"How long will I be on stand-by?"

As long as I am in uniform the airline personnel will try to find a place for me soon, but how soon?   These questions swirl around my head as we hustle through the crowd to arrange our ultimate destination.   My Grandmother's words play through my mind: "what a day of rejoicing that will be…"

The Trip of Trips

With very little leave accumulated, due to my emergency time required at home and our trip to Hawaii, we cannot plan a special get-away for a couple of months.   In the next few days I report in to Chief Nurse Pecora at Ft. McPherson, same song, second verse, only I do not feel like the same person who left from here a year ago.

Everyone seems glad that I am back stateside with no visible wounds.   My mother wants to feed me all the time because of my low weight.   I cannot eat much due to the mouth ulcers which heal with slow but steady progress.   Adjusting to new sleep patterns and eating habits evolve as the days pass. My body's circadian rhythm is off its axis. Jim and I adjust to our life together again. We question; we seek answers.   Was this the worst thing that could happen to us?   Will he have to go too?

I resume my duties as Head Nurse on the Women's Ward. We settle into a routine of work, drive, back to work. As thankful as I am to be stateside I cannot shake the heavy, sad feeling I have for those who are still in the struggle. And the war rages on.

In mid-February, thirteen U.S. helicopters went down in one day. During the last week of the same month U. S. troops begin the largest reported offensive campaign of the war, up near the Cambodian border. In March of 1967 the Viet Cong in the south ambush a U.S. truck convoy damaging 82 out of 121 vehicles. In the first week of April, the U. S. loses its 500th plane of the war. We fought back with jets' knocking out a power plant in Haiphong in North Vietnam.

About mid-April we begin thinking of taking some time away together. We both request leave for the first week in May. We read about the Expo '67 opening in Montreal.

"Sounds exciting but it will be a long trip." I say while we are having coffee one morning.

"Well, we have a good car. It'll be fun—and different. Plus, we can split the driving," counters Jim. This is his idea.

And so the plans begin!   We gather maps and information from various resources such as the Chamber of Commerce, the library, the television station.

Mother reminisces that she and dad went on their honeymoon to the World's Fair in New York in 1940.   My dad's mom accompanied them and they drove up in my mom's mother's car!

The World of Tomorrow

The theme was announced at its dedication by President Franklin Roosevelt on April 30, 1939.   They saw the beautiful crystal ball Perisphere and the impressive gold Trylon that were two featured structure of the fair.   On Constitution Mall stood a huge statue of George Washington while the Hall of Nations displayed the Soviet pavilion's statue of a worker hoisting a red star.   The Italian area showed a water-power generator.   Even though the official theme was progress and peace, mom says people were talking about the looming war in Europe.

One bright morning in May, armed with maps, lunch, snacks and clothing, we launch on our journey heading north, destination: Expo '67, Montreal, Canada.   We revel in each other's company, looking forward to our adventure. Our world seems on its axis again.

In April, the Viet Cong attacked Quangri and freed 200 prisoners.

The road seems longer and longer.   Jim drives, I sleep.   As we approach the Washington, D.C. area he decides that my turn to drive has come.   I try.   I struggle. Halfway into the Beltway, fight as I might, I am overpowered by the drowsiness.

"I thought the deal was to half up the driving," states Jim, sounding frustrated.

"Well I'm trying," I wail, "I just cannot keep my eyes open.   I think I have narcolepsy."

"Okay, okay, pull off at the next exit and we will switch--again," Jim snarls.

 In our attempt to save time and money we roll on at a steady pace.   After a nap, I do try to do some of the driving with better results. Late into the next afternoon we enter the Canadian border with no problem and head toward Montreal, our destination.   Dreary, rainy and cold is our first impression.

"Oh no," I groan, "I'm freezing, already.   I think I brought all the wrong clothes.   Here it is the first of May, supposed to be spring."

"You'll be alright once we start walking around," responds Jim, patting me on my knee.

After checking into our hotel and taking a short nap we decide to go check out the fairgrounds. "People, people everywhere," of all nationalities mill about with awed expressions. Colorful flags of all nations are snapping in the breeze. What a thrill to see the flame that was lit at the opening ceremony on April 27, still burning bright at the Places des Nations.

Somehow I do not think we will cover the 700 acres of exhibits, food vendors of all ethnicity and the very popular La Ronde amusement park. The largest exhibit, the Canadian complex, sprawls over a large area composed of a granite and steel structure, futuristic in design.

Some of the largest crowds teem in the vicinity of the United States lunar exhibit where a 123-foot-high escalator takes the brave ones by a simulated lunar landscape.

We decide to save that adventure for the next day so that we have time to experience some exotic cuisine. Besides, the cold is penetrating my inadequate clothing. I shiver and lean closer into Jim.

The next couple of days pass in a whirlwind of activity. We soon find ourselves on our return trip, headed south, with the promise of a sunnier, warmer climate.

My malaise continues, but I do log in some driving time since this part of the trip occurs during daylight hours.

Georgia and home never looked as good as when we roll across the state line then on toward Atlanta and the driveway of our little bungalow in Decatur. This trip allowed us plenty of time to talk in fact sometimes long into the night.   There were thousands of questions to be asked and answered.   There were also many moments of silence.

The Announcement

Diving back into the whirl of work with our different schedules makes time slip by unnoticed.   Though I still feel tired and a little nauseous at the smell of coffee I realize that several days have passed since my monthly cycle due date.   This being the second miss, I decide to call for an appointment at the Emory Clinic.   Surely, this must be just a fluke considering all our futile attempts in the past couple of years. We put the kibosh on perfect timing!

"All the signs are certainly there, Mrs. Brantley.   Now we have to wait for the test to return to confirm our examination," says Dr. Birch, "From the looks of everything your due date should be about December 28, a holiday baby.   Any questions?"

"No sir, not right now.   I'm sure I'll have plenty later."

"O.K., we will see you back here in a month. You know that you will see all of us in the clinic, so it won't be me every time.   That way, we are familiar with all our patients when we rotate call."

"Yes, I understand that.   Thank you."

After making my next appointment, I virtually danced and bounced on air leaving the office. Even though the final results were not in hand all signs pointed to a positive reading.   We were on our way toward fulfilling our next dream—to become parents.

"Yes, that's what he said after examining me and talking about my symptoms," I burbled to Jim over coffee in the hospital cafeteria.

Since he could not arrange to be there for my appointment, we decided that I should page him afterwards to talk, so here we are grinning at each other.   We decide to wait to announce our news until the test results confirm what I already feel.   Our secret will be difficult to keep.

Browsing through the baby department at Rich's, after leaving Jim to his work, I try to picture how our baby will look.

Hmm, probably will have brown eyes, after me, and brown hair from both of us.   This little white sweater will be good for a winter baby with dark coloring and this white blanket, so soft for cuddling.

I wonder if Rich's has a baby registry, like the bridal registry we were on a few years ago. We will need everything!

Over dinner that evening, I tell Jim about my stop at Rich's but assure him that I did not buy anything yet, just dreamed.   He listens, then reminds me that "he" needs something to sleep in first, like a crib, as well as diapers. Why does he have to be so practical?   I would rather have the blue suit or the white sweater first.

A Final Chapter,
A New Beginning

If one becomes pregnant while on active duty
it is up to the discretion of the Chief Nurse as
to whether the nurse can remain active, that is,
if she can continue to fulfil the duties as
assigned.   Since I need to work and my tour
of duty is not up until October, we decide that
I should try to complete my obligation to the
military.   None of this need be addressed
immediately as it is still early and I have no
symptoms other than mild nausea and malaise
which is under control and does not fall under
"need to know" information.

The long-awaited confirmation arrives:
positive!   Due date is approximately
December 28th.

As days turn into weeks so does my body
show changes in preparation for birth, such as
expansion and rounding in various places.

This morning I could hardly button the waist to my fitted Army-issue uniform. By the end of the day, I am feeling like ten pounds of potatoes stuffed into a five-pound sack. No uniforms are made for this. The time has come to improvise.

I still need to be able to wear the brass properly, that is, insignia and rank on the collar. We decide to try Jim's short-sleeved, white, button-up jacket with my uniform underneath, unbuttoned at the waist, with collar flipped out to properly hold the brass—perfect.

"Like your new uniform, Captain," chirped Sgt./ Jaynes, the wardmaster, as I walk into work this morning.

"Doing the best I can with what I'm dealing with, Sgt." I reply.

The day passes smoothly with only a few positive comments on my uniform change and no visit from the Chief Nurse. I figure as little attention drawn to it the better off I will be. It may not be government issue, but, the fit certainly feels better! Maybe those jungle fatigues can be an option for the later months.

As the days grow warmer and warmer my girth grows bigger and bigger and I grow hotter and hotter.   The more energy I exert the more difficult it is to breathe and stay cool. Will this summer never end?   Working in this old, sprawling building where the cool air comes from fans leaves one to wonder if the healing conditions are of the best quality. Would it "pass muster," to use an old military term?   Thus far, my makeshift uniform has caused no ruckus.

Finally, in late September, there comes a slight shift in the weather, a hint of fall in the air, a sign of some relief from the oppressive temperatures.

The ending date of my military career, October 7, 1967, now seems like a reality.

It occurs to me, however, that we will still need a second pay check in our household.   I decide to contact my former psychiatric nursing instructor who is now director of nursing at the Georgia Mental Health Institute. She agrees to hire me as a staff nurse upon my discharge from the military.   I make a plan to work up until two weeks before my due date, December 28th.

"So you are leaving the military due to your pregnancy, ma'am," asks the sergeant while typing away, not looking up.

"No, I'm leaving because I have fulfilled my obligation to the service, I am proud to say."

"Very good, ma'am, that's what I'll put on your discharge papers."

I walk out the door to begin the next chapter of my life, a different person than when I walked in.

Epilogue

In a discussion group, many years later, following a reading from my manuscript, a man commented with disdain, "some of us never went [to Vietnam]. Looks like you never left."

Taken aback by his barb, I just smiled and shook my head.

Later, as I thought about this remark, slung so carelessly at me, it occurred that, yes, I left there but it never left me.   It remains a part of who I am, a part of the fabric woven into my life.   It was not my choice to go but because I was there it affects the way I see the world and our country. I was forever changed.

In the words of Rose Kennedy, one of the great mothers of our time:

It has been said that time heals all wounds.   I do not agree.   The wounds remain.   In time, the mind, protecting its sanity, covers them with scar tissue, and the pain lessens, but it is never gone.

Little did I know that in less than twenty years I would again bring this motto into play...when Jim passed away.

CPSIA information can be obtained
at www.ICGtesting.com
Printed in the USA
LVHW092145270819
629196LV00001B/104/P